Lost and F

Don Howard

Foreword

Love and marriage has been the basis for a family life for most of us at some stage and for me it was no different. Unfortunately, I joined other poor souls in becoming divorced seven years later, and in my case leaving my two year old daughter Anneka with my ex-wife.

As the years rolled by and Anneka grew up we remained very close. When she was nearly twenty she asked me; "Dad, who were you before you met mum, what was your life?"

My heart sank from the bank of pain within me; these innocent questions hurt, and I had never felt the need to tell her my story.

I collected Anneka every other weekend and never realised we had a distance between us. My sadness fell all around me in many different currencies as I knew my funny stories and cheeky chappie experiences would have been told naturally over the years and would have been repeated often, I'm sure of it.

This is the time to tell all, but who would listen for more than ten minutes, I ask? No, I thought it had to be written down, and accurately too.

So here it is, my unique story from the age of three to eleven, with warts and all as they say. It's the tale of an independent little bugger who was never satisfied at being one amongst others. I was always off on a personal mission looking for adventure, well, every family's got to have one little sod within them!

Anneka,

This is probably the longest letter a father has ever written to his daughter, but I thought I should write down a few of Dad's tales for you to help you sleep! Regrettably, I was not blessed with the education required to write in complex verse and highfalutin text. I have, however, focused on keeping my writing as accurate and as interesting as possible. I have also remained observant and cautious of the ever present magnetism of self- indulgence.

My intention is to provide you with an insight of your Dad's life through some of the more interesting events and experiences, including the loves and losses I've had over the years. I realise some events may be a little dark for you but I am here to tell my story. I'm sure many children will have stories far more interesting than mine. But this is what happened to me, and maybe the next few pages will go a little way to explain Dad's madness and stupidly soft heart.

To help provide you with an insight of how my tales developed it may be worth noting that by the time I was eleven, I had attended twelve different schools and by the age of fourteen had lived in sixteen different places. The time my sister and I stayed in a children's home for a short period has not been included. Hectic early times for any child, and I hope you find the following pages as interesting and rewarding as I found the experience of living through them. I would change nothing, but given the choice to do it again, I wouldn't.

Contents

Early Days

I was born in Cornwall at a military hospital where my father, John Lewis Howard, was a signals technician in the Royal Air Force. He was stationed in Cornwall at RAF St Eval and was living in service quarters along with my mother Tia.

My mother was a very attractive young lady who was born in Holland during the war and was a year younger than my father.

After their romance started in Holland where my father was posted, my mother returned to England and they married in the UK. She fell pregnant with me eleven months later, and I came into this world during the festive Christmas period of 1959, only seven days before the big day itself. I must have been a fabulous gift to my young parents! Since that time I have been a charming gift to all those I have come in contact with. (*Would you look at that, a couple of lines and already I have succumbed to self- indulgence*)

My first ever memory has nothing to do with surviving photos of me as a young boy. Of these images I know nothing at all, even though they try desperately to convey their individual importance to me and perform a tantalising insight into my childhood, locked in a moment of time for all to see.

By the time I was sixteen months old I was living with my granny, as my mother was expecting again and was having a difficult time carrying her baby Marina, who was born on May fifteenth 1961.

When I was three, my father had left the air force and started work in Bletchley. We lived in a mid-terrace late Victorian house, halfway along a narrow road called Napier Street. Our houses were exactly the same design and style down both sides and all the way to the bottom; it was of a typical Victorian industrial town design. Our good fortune was at the end of our street where there was an open field that we often walked through. The actual house number was never known to me and, if it ever it was, I forget it now. I do however recall the colour of our front door. It was a dark maroon, like a 1930's tin of really dark red paint had been found in the shed and liberally used to cover its previous hideous green or maybe black covering. The house interior remains invisible to me except the kitchen and dining room.

One morning whilst my mother and I were standing in the kitchen doorway at Napier Street, a little hedge sparrow flew past us and straight into the kitchen via the open door. It flew frantically all around the room, trying to make its way back outside, but it soon panicked and became erratic in its behaviour. It found its way into the dining room. Although the little chap was clearly panicking, his measure of panic was nothing compared to what was coming to him. For in a few seconds of him being in the dining room he pooped on mother's tablecloth. Now my mother was more irritated and I could see the look on her face. She was having none of this anymore. She looked around for a stick or broom but she couldn't find one quickly enough so she grabbed my father's newspaper from the table and rolled it up tightly to make a policeman's truncheon.

The following action was fierce and brutal; her arms waving around like a deranged mourner at a funeral and her legs skitting from one direction to another without her feet seeming to leave the ground.
I never knew my mother was so agile and I was very impressed. After a few moments of her intense action, I also became as worried

for myself as the blows from the newspaper were many, without mercy to any young boy in the line of fire.

I watched helplessly as the bird flew towards the blue sky, but this ended with him crashing into the window panes and making an awful cracking sound as he would fly into them. He was a tough little feller; as every time he hit the window he would not fall, he kept in flight almost through the whole event. He did have a close shave when he clung onto a picture frame hanging on the back wall. This took a direct hit from the paper truncheon and so hung at a humorous angle for several days. The little bird made one last ditch attempt to escape the ferocious attentions of my enraged mother when it flew straight up the chimney. Regrettably this proved to be its downfall. "Gotcha" my mother shouted with loud excitement. I stood still next to the table watching her speaking to the little chap and trying to entice it down, she had a menacing and serious look on her face. "Come on little chap, come on" she would say whilst making the same finger gesture to it as she did me when I was summoned to be by her side.

I'm not sure how long it stayed up the chimney or how it managed to remain up there, but down it would have to come. It surely did, and after several tremendous swipes, my mother got it almost as soon as it flew out. My eyes could not believe all that had happened and my heart sank when I saw it lying on its back, wings out as if to demonstrate its dramatic demise to an audience. I watched her pick up its body, avoiding using her hands by un-rolling the paper truncheon which enabled her to use it as a flimsy shovel. It is here where I could use a little licence and say she presented the little chap to me with instructions to take care of its feathered and limp body to arrange its funeral and burial in the back garden. Alas, in honesty, without any regard to the creature's beauty, she tossed it into the dustbin and that was that. (*I prefer the garden bit!*)

***

A little way down the street from our house and on the other side lived one of my mother's newly made friends, whose name I can't recall. It was a family with three girls and one boy. I'm sure we were all between the ages of three and six. I only remember going to see them a few times and recall one visit that was to be very special to me. The inside of their house seemed to be the same as ours, rather plain and dull, though outside around the back they had a concrete pigsty, something I had never seen before and we didn't have. Their rear garden was very overgrown and out of bounds to us children. The adults told us it was impossible to play in it safely.

The day of note was the day my mother needed a long private conversation with the mother of this house, and while she was chatting and having a cup of tea, we kids were told to go play "hide-and-seek" upstairs so they could chat in peace. This instruction was eagerly undertaken by us all. This adventure resulted in my first sensitive experience, though I did not understand it at the time. I know three to four years old sounds a little uncomfortable but that is the first time for me.

I remember when the game started we were running about searching for suitable places to hide and after several rather poor attempts, I thought it would be a good idea to hide in their mother's double bed. I got into it and as I lay beneath the many woven blankets, I heard one of the daughters come into the same room and she was struggling to find somewhere to hide, I suggested she got in with me. She thought this was a good place too and we both giggled as we pulled the heavy covers back over the top of us. Whilst we were lying there together I held her close to me to make it look like there was only one person in the bed. In the semi-darkness I slowly became aware that it felt very nice holding her. I had never held anyone before, let alone a girl, as I had no need to. Lying next to her I started to feel nice and warm and had a sense of floating in a sea of warmth and cosiness. I began to wish we

8

wouldn't be found and so could lie here longer but it was soon over with a sudden eye aching brightness as the daylight came upon us again when the covers where pulled back to the call of "found you!"

We all scurried off and had to hide again but instead of the usual need and desire to find a better place, I was drawn back to the double bed. Off I went to hide in it again, and lay in the darkness as quiet as a mouse. I was alone; and although the previous warmth was now in my imagination I was sure I could still sense it from earlier. I was confused by my new feelings. I wasn't interested in the game anymore I was only thinking of being back into the nice warm space again with the girl who had hidden with me. That was a much better plan, I got out the bed and ran out of time to hide so was soon caught out. Brilliant, I thought to myself as I went to find the same girl and quickly suggested we hide in the double bed again, she thought that was a good place too. I was very excited and we soon resumed our place beneath those heavy covers. I suggested we lay together again and she agreed. This time I held her close and found within myself a growing and uncontrollable desire to hold her a little more tightly. I find it a little difficult to consider, but I may have also moved a little as well. Whatever safety mechanisms girls and women have built-in for situations like this it must be in place at birth for in a flash she was out of that bed faster than a fireman on call.

Though we were both about four, I had just experienced something wonderful and enjoyable a feeling never experienced before and that remains with me to this day. I also experienced my first conscious feeling of embarrassment and maybe a little shame. The girl now kept herself away from me and we never hid together again. It's nice to know that of all the things we forget I always recall her long brown hair and her pretty face.

My mother and I did go back to that house on occasions, but we never played "hide-and-seek" again, and for that matter I don't recall seeing the girls either, for I think the parents had split up. That was my life in Bletchley, apart from a few trips out, sitting in a wooden cart my father had made for this purpose and him pulling my sister and I around the field at the end of our street.

* * *

 Soon afterwards, we moved a few miles out of Bletchley to a little village called Deanshanger. It was a pleasant place and fairly modern in comparison to the adjacent village of Stony Stratford with its lovely old stone bridge. We had a brand new semi-detached house, very light and spacious inside and very modern on the outside. It looked fabulous to me, and had lots of green grass all around it. With no walls or fencing it had a real sense of freedom about it. There were wide roads and other new modern houses around us; some still under construction. Little did I know this house would be hell on earth for my mother and I.

First School

My father had little to do with us children. Of course he was working, but before and after work he always seemed to disappear. My father never showed any paternal feelings nor demonstrated any paternal actions of kindness and affection to my sister and I that I am able to recall. One day, my mother was showing me how to tie my shoe laces so I could do it for myself at school. He stood in the doorway and told her to show me one more time and then to leave me on the settee until I could do it, and she was told not to show me again. I was not allowed off until I could demonstrate to him I could do them, and I eventually did learn that same day. But it was mainly our mother who took control of what we did and when we did it. For instance, I remember my mother taking me in the morning to my new school for the first day.

I had put on my new clothes and tied my shoes myself! She took me by the hand and walked me all the way so I would know the way myself the next day. As we made our way we passed some council houses, my mother asked me never to go inside these houses because the people who lived there might kill you! She always said stark and shocking things to us with great effect. When we arrived at my new school we were shown to the classroom that was to become mine. We both approached the door and mother knocked gently on the door.

The lady teacher looked at us and smiling politely invited us both in. We joined her at her desk and she pointed to an empty chair and desk for me to sit at. As I let go of my mother's warm and firm grip and nervously walked in and took my seat. All the children's heads were transfixed at different angles from their bodies whilst looking at me. Was the interest in me because I was new or was it that I had not been killed when walking past the council houses? The teacher was showing me signs of understanding from where she was sitting. A little later she came over and very softly spoke to me to get me to stop crying, as I had been since my mother had left the room. I eventually settled down. I wasn't listening to the teacher. Instead I was looking out the windows, reflecting on my walk to school that morning and the things I had seen.

Earlier, we had walked past a large farmyard with an interesting collection of stone buildings within its high walls. This farm was all I could think about during my first day at my new school. Later when my mother came to collect me I was keen to go, but more important to me was me being able to look inside the farmyard again. I was fascinated by the farm for the duration of my time at the school and I was equally fascinated with a stream that ran through the massive trees in the surrounding area.

***

There has to a first time for everything we do and this day was to be my first day of several truants. I was finding it difficult to settle down, as the other children had already made themselves into little groups and I found it hurtful when I was excluded. I found it easier just to walk about by myself and hope for another new boy to join this school, then I could help him settle in. (*Talk about the blind leading the blind*)

I started to develop a desire to write my name; at first secretly on my desk, then the window sills and later a little less discreetly on the brickwork. I was fed up of being invisible to the other children in the classroom at school, and wanted my name and hopefully myself to be noticed.

Eventually one of the teachers called me over and told me, "It's best if you stop writing your name on the walls, this is not that sort of school." Now it looked like the teachers disliked me also, so I thought 'right, I'm off tomorrow.'

When the next day came I was very happy and excited as I knew I would not be in the school with that problem again. Oh no, I would be off finding stuff in the fields and climbing trees. Maybe I would follow the stream for as far as I dared. I walked down to the school with the other children and carefully passed the council houses, ready to run at a moment's notice. Down and over the bridge that crossed the stream, past the farm yard I liked so much and towards my school. As the other children and parents in front of me turned right, then went on through the school gates, I did not. No, I just carried walking on and passed with my head held high as if I had a purpose. Nobody said a word, so I walked and walked. I loved it, freedom and the wind blowing in to my face with the birds singing in those large trees. This was so much better.

An hour or so later I was sitting on the kerb on the side of the road, watching the cars and trucks go by and feeling a little hungry. Without any warning I was pulled up from the roadside by the tops of both my ears. It was bloody agony and I had no time to think or react. In one split second I was day-dreaming and the next was standing on my tip toes yelling in pain "What the hell..."

Then I recognised the voice! It was my mother; she had been on one of the buses that had driven past when she thought she recognised a boy sitting on the road side. Then the penny dropped that it was me. She pressed the stop button on the bus and got off, making her way to me unnoticed. Well, by now the consequences of my actions were starting to become a little harsher.

Rabbits & Motorbikes

My father had taken a job at the Vauxhall motor factory in Luton, Bedfordshire. Years later my mother told me that because my father was an educated and proud man, his job in the factory was getting him down. It must have been hard for him seeing all those new cars every day and doing nothing more interesting than putting wheels on them as they went by on the production line. We didn't have a car then, so we never went out unless we used the bus.

However, my father did have a Honda 90cc motorbike to ride to work and back on. I recall it was a bright red one with a cream plastic front leg guard. I thought it looked smashing. Once he took me and my sister out on it to the next town, though we never arrived. I remember this outing on his motorbike very clearly because he rode it through a car park to cut a corner in an attempt to avoid a red traffic light, but unfortunately rode straight into a large pothole which jilted the bike so much that my sister fell off the back.

I was more fortunate because I was holding on to him. Really, my sister, being eighteen months younger than me should have been in the middle, but this was not my decision to make. Unfortunately for Marina, when I informed my father that she had fallen of the back he seemed to ignore this information. If it hadn't been for me shouting and protesting to the best of my ability, along with onlookers waving him down, I don't know when he would have taken any notice of me. He eventually stopped and looked back. Marina was crying in the arms of a lady who was furious with my father. Not only had she fallen off the bike, she had no helmet and had received a massive raw burn to her inner thigh that was a horrible sight to behold, let alone being the victim of the painful injury!

***

Whilst we lived at this house in Deanshanger, my sister and I had a grey pet rabbit each. Mine was called Ben, be it a girl or a boy, and Marina's was called Queenie. We never made much fuss of them and didn't really take much of an interest. That was until one morning when they had both disappeared!

They had escaped, was the explanation from my mother. "Escaped?" I asked rather alarmed. But why? They had food and water the odd carrot and lettuce leaf that I had on occasion pushed through the mesh myself. And anyway, how could a rabbit get its furry paws through the wire mesh and undo the lock? "Well, it did", was the abrupt reply and within seconds my sister and I both broke down in tears. A few minutes later my salty tears had gone and my red eyes could see the face of my mother and sister again. I bravely advised my mother and sister that I would go out and find both rabbits, no matter how long it would take me, and bring them home.

Amazingly, she let me go off down the street with my sister in tow. We walked some distance around the estate and eventually came out onto the main road. It was on a stretch of that road I chanced upon a dead traffic squashed rabbit.

"This is Ben," I explained to my tentative sister,
"Is it?" she cried.

"Yep!" I said, "No doubt about it."

Marina replied "but its squashed flat". My sister was distraught at this sight, "So is it my rabbit or yours?" she asked through her tears. I felt so sorry for her I came up with a solution to pacify her. I told Marina that I knew a place where I could take the dead rabbit to under the nearby hedge where a man would save it and bring it back to life. But when he did this the rabbit would be forbidden to go back into its cage. Instead it would have to fend for itself in the open fields within the surrounding countryside. Marina paused for a while and then eagerly bought into the idea, much to my relief.

It was now my task to uplift the flattened critter from the road; a task I was far from capable of doing. I came up with yet another suggestion. I informed Marina I was not permitted to touch the rabbit as the Hedge man was the only person with the gift of life and he would do the good deed under the cover of darkness, but assured her that I would come back in the morning to make sure the hedge man had taken his duties seriously and freed our rabbit to the green and rolling countryside all around us.

I made several scooter rides during that week and would often make a small detour to see if the rabbit had gone. I didn't want Marina knowing I had deliberately misled her. She had already been expressing her doubts as to whether or not this was one of our rabbits.

***

It was around this time I had my first experience of foolishness, or possibly spitefulness. I would be terribly ashamed if it showed me being spiteful. One Sunday afternoon, Marina and I went for a stroll around our estate looking for an adventure to appear before our very eyes. It was a nice spring day with the sun shining and clear blue skies, though a little chilly. As we strolled along, throwing stones and rocks at people's fences and gates, we came upon a place where the builders had parked some of the site machinery and equipment. I noticed all these machines had been painted in a dull yellow, it seemed a girly colour to me, and I wondered why yellow?

We both ran over to see what fun we could have with these big yellow machines. After a while of scurrying around them I decided I must climb up onto each and every one of them to see if I could get into the drivers cabs of the few that had them. This was to be my adventure of the day and I wanted Marina to enjoy the thrill with me. I was in my element here. I took Marina by the hand and set off to the nearest dirty yellow machine. I had an energy and determination to climb onto each and every one to provide me with the adventure I was seeking and the satisfaction of achievement.

My thinking was the bigger and dirtier the machine the better for me. First was a dumper truck, incredibly dirty, though still yellow. I could clearly see it had been severely bashed about. Each dent and mangled metal panel or bracket was an untold story to me, and enhanced the thrill of my being on this four wheeled mechanical dirt mover. I can see it now, and can still smell its engine, that was black with old oil combined with dirt and an intoxicating smell of leaking diesel. It was all over the engine and had dripped through its chunky frame down on to the soil beneath.

The engine was a scary looking lump of mighty complexity with many nuts and bolts holding it together, wires, springs, levers and buttons everywhere, and all covered in a mixture of thick black oil, dirt and pink diesel; even at my young age I could sense this stuff was the last thing my mother would want me to come home with on my clothes or me. But getting on the dump truck and avoiding the oil and grime seemed possible enough, if we were careful and mindful of the consequences!

Once aboard the dump truck, I just had to sit in the driver's chair. It was black and torn to shreds. No arm rests, just a basic chair, though to me the man who sat here was as sophisticated as any airline pilot. This was my moment to become the magnificent driver and controller of the beast I was sitting on. I sat in the chair and grabbed the large and surprisingly thin steering wheel with the intention to turn it left and right at my whim. It was a shame I couldn't turn it more than an inch or so, and the reality was disappointing to say the least as I had absolutely no control at all, not even the basics in turning the steering wheel. After pushing and pulling a few levers I got bored and jumped off and we made our way to some other machines. With my excitement now slowing down we made our way back home via a different path, one I had not walked before but could tell it was going to get us home.

Whilst we walked along I could see in front of us a large cutting into the soil next to the path. It looked like the builders had dug out the bank to park some more machines in, and our path ran down the bank alongside the cutting to the road at the bottom. When we got to the cutting I could see the rain from previous days had collected in the top end about four inches or so. The cutting was about a metre's drop to the bottom from the path where we both stood. As we stood together and for no good reason, I nudged Marina and she fell into the cutting, getting soaked in the water and covered in dirt. What a little sod I was, and how bloody spiteful was that! I looked at her as she lay in the dirty water. "Oh shit," I thought and ran down to help her up. I did my best to clean her up and to stop her crying, and although she wasn't hurt she was very upset from falling off the edge and ending up on her bottom in mud.

Unbeknownst to me a lady had been watching us whilst walking alone down the path and had witnessed me and my stupid action. She quickly came running over to help sort things out. She checked Marina over to make sure she was unharmed and then gave me a right telling off. "You stupid little sod," she yelled, holding my arm and shaking me, "You bloody stupid little sod," again she shouted "you could have hurt your sister!" She then smacked me around the head and asked where we lived so she could take us both safely home. Oh boy was I in for it now! Marina would not stop crying and we were getting closer and closer to our home. I had to minimise the negative situation by somehow getting Marina to stop crying. I

19

tried everything, joking, telling jolly tales and pulling twisted faces, but to no avail.

Marina told me she was terrified of what was going to happen to her when mum saw the state she was in. I thought for a moment and came up with a story to fix the situation. I told Marina that this lady who was taking us home was also going to take us to a shop where the owner was known to her and had a special washing machine that could wash and dry children, enabling her to walk out as if nothing had happened. She doubted me at first, but I continued to assure her it was all good and had been tested to work really well and she would be amazed at the results. Eventually she believed me and stopped crying just in time.

I was however, badly mistaken in my belief that I had mitigated my wrongdoing and maybe my punishment, for when we arrived home the lady clearly presented to my mother a full and descriptive re-enactment of what she saw. My mother showed me the power of learning through physical punishment.

***

I must have a selfish side as well, for another event involving my sister clearly sits uncomfortably within my memory. It was Christmas Eve and I remember feeling the excitement all youngsters must have when they first consciously realise what Christmas could bring to them. I went to bed but was unable to sleep, though the house was warm and decorated in accordance with the season. The tinsel and charms hanging on the tree were hanging low waiting for Father Christmas, so if I could stay awake I would hear the charms on the tree move and jingle or the sound of the tinsel slipping to the floor as he placed my presents beneath the Christmas tree I had helped to decorate.

For some reason, my sister was in the same bed as me, and she was sound asleep. My father came upstairs and explained why I should sleep and not become a bad boy or Father Christmas would pass me by. Mother came up the stairs and say much the same until eventually I slipped off, never to hear the telling sounds I was so determined to hear.

Very early that Christmas morning, maybe around six or so, I awoke. I looked around me and saw nothing on the floor or window sill, then I noticed at the bottom of the bed was a pillow case containing some presents and a large old hiking sock hanging on the bed. I could clearly make out there was an apple and maybe an orange inside the sock. I looked over to my sister who was still asleep.

I was just about to wake her up when I noticed something was wrong. Wait a minute I thought, there was only one pillow case and only one sock. Well if I'm not having the sock that must be Marina's so I grabbed the pillow case and started to plunder its contents. I'll have a doll, don't see any harm in that, I thought as it began to appear from the wrapping paper. A coat that won't fit me and is in a girls colour isn't so bad! At this point Marina was awake and sitting up looking a little upset as she seemed to have nothing from Father Christmas except an old sock with fruit in it.

I could clearly see the insensitivity in what I was doing but no way was I going to have nothing, even if Marina was crying. Marina's crying soon received the swift attention of both parents and they appeared in the doorway. Marina was immediately reacquainted with her gifts from Father Christmas and still had a few additional ones to open herself, though neither of us managed to avoid the fruit because we had a sock each. One sock had fallen on the floor.

My pillow with its wrapped contents intact had been hidden under the bed, as they thought I would wake in the night and open mine without sharing the experience, as I most likely would have done.

Apparently two pillow cases full of presents and two children all in a single bed Christmas would not have worked for my parents. They were right, so why not keep them all out of sight until they were ready. No boy is going to take notice of his sister's name on the only pillow case in his room full of presents! When Marina had stopped crying she was invited to help me open my presents. Aren't parents clever things at times! I was told off, and so I should have been! (*Little sod*)

One of my gifts that year was a torch that had a coloured lens on the end, allowing me to change the colour of light. It was brilliant fun and I played with it every night for ages. I also received a cloth roadway design about one and a half metres square. I could lay it down on the living room floor, unroll it and drive my cars and trucks around. But the torch was my favourite gift, and soon to be my undoing. Sometime after Christmas I had the torch in hand and was getting bored. What I needed was somewhere dark to see the colours again, as in the daylight it was pretty rubbish. I went into mum's bed room and opened her wardrobe door.

My mother's wardrobe was an old massive brown one. It had two large doors, one had a mirror on the inside, and the other some rails for ties. One half was full of long dresses and coats, and the other side had shirts hanging from a rail, then a shelf with several fitted drawers below. I decided to keep the door closed on the side with the coats, and that I would climb up onto the shelf with the shirts above and close the door to be able to use the torch in the dark. All seemed good to me the problem was as I couldn't get up on the shelf easily neither could I get down without hanging on to the rail that the shirts hung on.

After a fashion, I eventually found a way to get into the wardrobe and up onto the shelf. Now I could have the fun with the torch I had expected in the dark with the doors closed. It was enchanting. After a while I got fed up so decided to get out and do something else. I un-latched the door and pushed it open, it swung right out and away from me, then I put the torch into my trouser back pocket and held onto the shirt rail to swing out of the cupboard.

This is when it all went horribly wrong, for as I swung out of the cupboard it felt to me as the floor of the bedroom had been lifted and was making its way straight towards me and in an instant I was back in total darkness with the noise of breaking glass all around me and the sound of falling debris, then silence. Not a sound. What on earth had happened, I had no idea.

I was dazed and confused and in an uncomfortable position. I soon realised the cupboard had fallen on top of me. I tried to push the cupboard up and away from me, but it was useless as I didn't have the strength.

I banged on the sides, calling for help, and eventually heard my mother coming into the bedroom gasping at what she saw. The wardrobe was no longer standing upright how it should be, oh no, it was laying down on its front with the doors closed. She knew it was me inside, and must have wondered herself what the hell was happing. When she heard me explain I was stuck in the wardrobe and asked her to get me out. She was shocked and asked, strangely enough, "What are you doing in there?" Isn't it funny the things we can say in a crisis?

No matter how hard she tried to lift the thing up and off me she was unable to, so she advised me to "Wait a minute!" while she went next door to get help. Within no time at all a neighbour had come to the rescue and I was freed to walk straight into my mother's swinging right hand. "You wait till your father gets home", a delightful phrase my mother was always keen to threaten me with. I was used to hearing it and the consequences. A smack in the face or on the legs was to be avoided wherever possible, but grounding was the worst for me. I was always out of the house climbing trees and doing general boy stuff. The wardrobe incident entitled me to be grounded for a couple of days and all the weekend, with no TV to watch either.

By Saturday afternoon I was so desperate to get out the house I remember opening my mother's bedroom window and climbing onto the window sill. I sat with both my legs dangling freely outside, and I was swinging them from side to side scrapping the heel of my shoes against the brickwork. I was trying to calculate the distance to jump and whether I should chance it.

The only other option was to climb fully out of the window and lower myself down, hanging on the outside window ledge by my fingertips in an attempt to reduce the distance of the drop. I was ninety percent sure I could do either successfully. Luckily for me, I chose to sneak out of the back door when My Mother popped down to the shops, as I knew she wouldn't be back for around half an hour. A much better decision, you may think. As it turned out, it wasn't.

My intention was to pop out undetected, have some fun and return with my mother none the wiser. This seemed very exciting and would offer me the satisfaction of having the last laugh. I made sure she was out of sight and well on her way before I opened the kitchen door and made a bolt for it. As I ran towards the playing field I could hear other children playing around the massive white water tower just down the road from our house. I changed direction and rushed on to investigate.

The water tower had a security fence all around it. It was a green wire mesh type and about six feet high with concrete support posts every fifteen feet or so. The kids had broken through the mesh fencing and where messing up the place. Some of the boys were busy writing graffiti on the walls, using stones and the dirt that was all around them. The other boys threw rocks at the glass windows and I could see that some had been smashed. This was not my sort of fun and I told the lads to stop doing what they were doing, or they would get themselves into a lot of trouble. One of the tough boys told me to bugger off, and another one shouted at me and then went inside the tower through the door that someone had broken down.

I was horrified that these lads where so bad and were running amok. A voice called to me from above. No, not God! But some big bully of a lad who was on top of the tower swearing down to me to "something- off" and I noticed standing next to him was the same boy I had seen running into the tower a few seconds earlier. As I made my way out of the compound I was struck on the head by what I thought was a dead bird that had hit me beak first. I turned around and looked up I saw the two boys on the tower throwing stuff down at me.

It was not heavy stones, as I first feared, but shards of broken glass from the windows smashed in the water tower. Without any warning the glass was coming down on me thick and fast. I was too proud to run, so I walked calmly away with one hand holding my head. As I reached the hole in the fence, I felt the blood came pouring down the right side of my face from above my ear, and when I was out of sight I started to run home fast to sort things out as best I could.

On my way a man caught hold of me to offer some help so I started explaining to him what had happened, and where. I then pulled away and made off home. The rest of the story is as you would expect. Mum came home and saw the blood on me and my clothes. Our neighbours took me somewhere to have my head looked at, resulting in a couple of stitches. Later that evening the man who had stopped to help me came round to our house with one of the big boys. He forced this lad to apologise to me and my parents. That's fine, I thought, but it did not put right the bollocking and cuffing I had received from my father. The point of this tale is that this always seemed to be the way things turned out for me, two steps forward and one back!

Discipline and punishment in our home was a way of life and both were given with enthusiasm and in equal measure. I do not recall what my punishment was on all occasions, but maybe that's just as well.

Safe Refuge

During our time at the house in Deanshanger my mother and father always seemed to be arguing. During the latter time they would physically fight with each other so often that Marina and I would have to go to a house just across the road. I will always remember the two dear old sisters who must have been in their seventies, together in what soon became our safe house. They had a lovely bungalow with soft furnishings and floral wallpaper. They had many different plants in pots strategically placed around their home. They must have been there for some time, for nearly everybody would stop when passing to talk to them if they were out tending to their colourful gardens. In later years I wish I had the presence of mind to visit them and thank them for all they did for us, and the many sweets and cakes my sister and I consumed whilst under their care.

When these two ladies would hear the shouting start – and maybe plates being smashed, who knows – they would always come over together and ask mum if they should take Marina and I to their house until things had settled down.

Sometimes when the two ladies came to collect us my father would shout and swear at them but they kept their heads down, and tightly holding our hands just kept walking up the garden path, never looking back and telling us not to look back either. My mother was always grateful for their help and afterwards would take us around to them and sit have a cup of tea, until the next time when it all kicked off again.

One very clear memory I have of these times was hearing my mother and farther arguing loudly in the hall way. The arguing became more intense and aggressive and my father stood in the way of the front door and refused to let us through. When his guard was down, somehow my mother managed to seize the opportunity and forcefully push him outside the front door onto the garden path where I saw him fall to his knees and roll into a dishevelled heap of arms and legs. For a moment I found this funny. I know it sounds out of context, but I did. Mum took advantage of his plight and quickly locked the door before he could get back in. He started raging and thumping the door so hard we thought he would break it down.

My mother pushed us into the kitchen, as we could not get out of the front door to the two old ladies across the road this time. This was it, my sister and I were in this together with our mother and we had no idea what to expect or do, or how to help our mum who was beginning to look desperate herself.

My sister and I opened the inner kitchen door to watch the commotion, and suddenly our mother pushed through us in a blind panic, "He's running around the back" she screamed "quick, stop him getting in," What, I thought, me stop him? As Marina and I looked on, to our horror my mother and father both got to the rear kitchen door at the same time. Now I was really scared, for I could clearly see the rage in his eyes and the bulbous veins running along the sides of his forehead. Again, my mother's quick action and swift thinking got the better of him. She managed to click the lock down just as, in the same instant, he lunged at the door handle.

He was hopping mad, shouting and spitting on the ground; his teeth constantly gripped shut as if they had been glued together. Then it all went very quiet, not a sound from outside. The three of us cautiously made our way to the kitchen window and peered outside to see where he had gone but he was not there. We went to the living room window and the same, he was nowhere to be seen. The tension was shifting from possible violence to something that seemed even more terrifying, the unknown.

The suspense was soon broken when I heard a sound coming from the downstairs toilet. I gently crept along the burgundy carpeted hallway and tentatively opened the toilet door with my head tilted sideways. I peered through the gap in horror with my eyes now resembling a startled owl. I saw my father trying to climb through the partially opened window. I slammed the door shut and shouted to mum, and as she came rushing to me I explained "its dad, he's trying to force open the window more as he can't get through it."

Mum opened the door and saw him stuck in the window holding a long piece of wood. To my amazement my mother did not shut the door on him. Instead she walked in and just stood there, hands on her hips, shouting at him.

I was a little confused as she seemed quite confident with the situation, as if somehow she now had the upper hand. Unknown to me, at that moment in time she did. He was actually stuck halfway through the damn window. It shouldn't have been funny but somehow it was bloody hilarious! Mum eventfully closed the door on him, leaving him in the window and telling us she was taking us across the road. That was fine for us, but I was begging my mother to come over with us. I feared for her, and was upset at having to leave her behind.

I was about to discover that you should never underestimate a woman's capabilities. As we made our way to the front door, my mother stopped in her tracks and dashed into the under stairs cupboard and came out with dads hammer. Yes, his hammer. "Oh gosh, what on earth is she going to nail down or nail closed now," I thought. "Surely it's best if we just run to the bungalow across the road," but my mother had other ideas.

After unlocking the front door and leaving it open, she walked us back into the hallway. This seemed to be taking us away from the exit to safety when surely we should be running out and up the road away from him. She held our hands and took us with her to the downstairs toilet door my father was still behind. She then opened the toilet door fully and stepped inside, just a few feet away from him, whilst he was still struggling to free himself from the window frame. My nervous mother told him she was going to call the police this time in an attempt to stop him being so angry with her. He just started shouting and making more threats of what he was going to do to her when he got in the house.

My mother shouted back at him and then started swearing in his face. Then in full view of my sister and me, as he angrily responded to her barrage of verbal abuse, she raised her right hand that was holding his hammer and brought it quickly down, striking him full force on the head. He looked at her and with his eyes filled with intense rage lunged at her with both his hands. My mother raised her arm again and struck his head a second time with the hammer! He slumped onto the basin below the window and started moaning and groaning. My mother let the hammer slip from her hands onto the toilet floor and walked out.

She grabbed our hands and we all ran to the open front door, making a dash for it, leaving the door open as we ran. We quickly reached the ladies in the bungalow, who had come outside. Before we went in we looked back at our house and saw my father fall disgracefully from the toilet window and lie on the grass holding his head in his hands.

It wasn't long before he came banging on the doors of the house where we were now hiding. I remember the two old ladies trying to talk to him quietly through the door in an attempt to calm him down. Their tone soon changed when he came banging and staring at them through the big windows they had. "Welcome to our world," I thought. Thankfully the police arrived shortly and that was the end of the day's antics.

The worst thing to happen to me was not long after the hammer incident. All I remember is one minute I was crying upstairs in my bed and my father shouting to me to shut up from downstairs. Suddenly with no indication that anything bad was about to happen to me, my father burst into my room, ripped off my bed covers and grabbed me by the hair, taking me to the landing. He started shouting at my mother to help shut me up or he would throw me over the banister. I could see my mother downstairs and watched her plead with him to let me go, but to no avail. She began to make her way up the stairs to rescue me when my father shouted at her to stop and go back down again.

At that moment he let go of my hair and picked me up by twisting my pyjamas on my back and bottom. He then turned me upside down and, holding me by the ankles, held me over the banister so I was facing my mother. He shouted at her and told her that if she didn't go back down the stairs he would let me go and "kill the little bastard!"

We all knew he was not messing around and he would drop me. My mother went back down the stairs, crying like I had never seen her cry before. After a few seconds she fell to her knees and clasped her hands together as if she was at a church service. She begged my father to please hold on and place me back into my bed, where she would make me go to sleep. After a moment's stand-off, I was being taken by my ankles still upside down, down the stairs and dropped onto the floor in front of my mother. My mother pulled me on her lap and tightly hugged me whist we cried for ages. I can only thank her, for he eventually came to his senses and did the right thing. Soon after this incident my parents split up.

***

31

My sister and I had to live with my father's mum, Granny Pole, for a time. We had no idea what was happening to us and I don't recall being bothered by it either. We were now going to be living with granny for a while. She lived just outside Bletchley in a village called, Loughton on Shenley Church End, in the second Victorian semi at the bottom of London Road and almost on the corner of Shelly Road. Granny's house seemed to offer me plenty of opportunities for possible adventure.

Granny had a massive coal shed made out of railway sleepers, can you believe it. No sooner had we moved in, I found the coal shed irresistible and just had to play in the coal amongst all the soot and large lumps of black rock, I now loved the smell of coal and it was magical to me. Even more fascinating to me was that some lumps of coal had hundreds of beautiful gold specks within them. I would smash them to pieces to get the gold out but was never able to collect it adequately. My granny was a typical white haired lady. She was tall, and always walked with her back straight, had a big bosom and seemed to be always cooking something. If it wasn't rhubarb on the boil it could be beetroot on the boil or maybe her clothes boiling and simmering away in the copper next to her Belfast sink.

Her dinners where always dished up onto her collection of faded pale blue willow pattern plates. She was a kind lady to me and my sister whilst we stayed there, and we would get away with everything.

It was not the same story for her children, Granny would often tell me her stories of bringing up three naughty boys and how she would have no fooling about and would be very strict with them and still was. When my father was a boy he and his two brothers Michael and Norman would live in fear of the brown leather belt that granny had hooked to the back of her dining room chair. It was often used, from stories gleaned from gran, on my father and his brothers.

Granny was married twice and her second husband was a man called Bert; he was not my dad's father. Gran had re-married in the sixties. Bert was a quiet man but as strong as oxen, he used to be a stoker on the steam trains and worked out of Bletchley station. Now he seemed to never leave his arm chair, he would sit in it hour after hour watching the horse racing and the weather programmes on the telly. I used to watch him make paper twists for lighting the fire with. He would make half a dozen at a time and place them into an old jar next to the fire so they were always at hand when the fire needed to be lit.

The move to Granny's must have been very soon after Christmas, for my uncle Michael had brought round two presents for me. One was the biggest present I had ever seen, let alone received. He used to smoke a pipe and always used Golden Virginia tobacco, which came in a smart green and gold tin, similar in size to a cigarette packet though maybe a little larger. He had been collecting these tins all year and had placed them neatly into a large cardboard box covered in Christmas wrapping paper.

The box contained maybe fifty tins or so. My uncle explained to me they could be used to build all sorts of things, however, one tin has a surprise contained within it and the item was wrapped in cotton wool so as not to be discovered too early. I then had to open each tin until I found my prize. It turned out to be a well-polished half-crown coin, (*why do I wish I hadn't told you that!*) in those days it was worth two and a half shillings whatever that is today I have no idea!

I was so pleased with those tins, I could not stop playing with them. But unbeknownst to me, my father was becoming agitated and jealous of the fun I was having. He told me to put them all away until another time. My uncle protested and said that as I was having such fun I should be allowed to continue playing with them, but to no avail, and my father insisted I put them away. This disagreement was still bubbling under the surface between the two brothers as we sat at granny's table for dinner and later spilled out when I was playing with the second present my uncle Michael had given me.

My second present was a pair of pistols, black sucker pistols that fired a plastic bolt with a red sucker on the end. It came complete with six suckers and a tin target the size of a dinner plate. My uncle showed me how to load the pistols and how to hold them so I could fire straight at the target. We were having great fun when my uncle suggested I should go to the top of Granny's stairs and he would sit at the bottom and we could fire the suckers at each other for some daring and scary fun.

Wow! I thought, this sounds like the best fun ever and in a flash I was running up the stairs to take up my position. We had a great time laughing together and shooting each other. What could have been more fun for any boy? Eventually my father came into the hallway to see what we were getting all excited about.

He explained that although it looked like fun, it was dangerous and we should go back to shooting at the target provided with the pistols. Uncle Michael tried to reason with him that a little risk was what most fun was, and after a few words were exchanged my father came up the stairs to take the pistol away from me.

It was at this point my uncle shot at him with his pistol; it hit my father in the chest so my father shot him back with my pistol and so it went on for a few shots until my father was shot in the face! An argument ensued and my gran came into the stairway to try to sort them both out. She was unable to do anything except get me out of the way and back into the sitting room after closing the door on them. We could now hear them fighting. When they eventually came back into the living room they looked a right sight. And that spoiled everything for ages, because the tobacco tins and the set of pistols were never seen again.

***

The only recollection I have of my sister during this time was when my granny was telling her off. Marina had a doll she called Daisy, and one day my granny was watching Marina from the corner of her eye because she had sneaked a small pair of scissors from Gran's sewing basket.

She hid them in her dress, took them outside and sat on the step in the front door porch. My gran was intrigued to see what she was up to and so went into the front living room where the bay fronted window overlooked the front door and porch. Marina could be seen sitting on the doorstep with her doll and for reasons known only to Marina, began to pushing the scissors into Daisy's plastic body, making several holes in her.

My Gran was astonished and confused by Marina's actions. Then Marina got up off the step and walked calmly round the house to the rear and into the kitchen where Granny was waiting for her. "Well," said Granny, "What have we here?" she gently asked Marina. Marina started to cry and explained that she had just found Daisy on the step at the front door and that Don must have done it! Maybe she remembered me nudging her into the dirt and this was payback time. Bless her, whatever her intentions were, all she got was a right telling off and a lot more tears.

We hadn't noticed it, but a few weeks had passed and we hadn't seen our mother since arriving. It only came to my attention because one afternoon there was a lot of talk about her within the house, and a hurried look on people's faces who were constantly looking out of the windows. I heard things like, "she's not coming in here" and "I'll deal with it, she won't get past me", and so on. The tension was building and Granny and Bert were talking to my uncle Norman when the next thing, all hell broke out.

I saw my mother coming past the rear window and Granny dashing outside to engage with her. The conversation looked hostile, and although I had no knowledge of the details it all looked very threatening to my mother. I made a move to go to her and my uncle got hold of me by the arm just as I almost reached her by the back door. Now my uncle was shouting at her as well as my granny, mum was crying but I did not know why they would not let her into see me or let Marina and me out to see her. By now my uncle had a firm grip on me as I was struggling to break free to be with my mother or help her somehow. I was not sure what I could do but I now wanted to run away with my mum.

Things took a turn for the worse for my mother. Bert, who had been mouthing off abuses at my mother from the comfort of his threadbare arm chair, pulled himself out of it and stomped across the living room like a crazed demon. The brute pushed passed me and then savagely grabbed my mother's long black hair and pulled her head down so it was in-line with her stomach. He then brutally started shaking her as he dragged her around the side of the house. My mother was trying to get a better position and at the same time trying without any success to release herself from this man's powerful grip. She was screaming in pain and desperation calling for someone to help her, but nobody would. He continued dragging her in the same awkward manner and still by the hair. Not once did they think about us children, crying as we watched this awful scene before us.

Along the front path they both went, and when they reached the front gate he swung it open with his other hand and literally threw my mother out into the street regardless as to the possibility of on-coming traffic. My mother fell and rolled into the middle of the road, she looked like a traffic accident. When she first attempted to stand, he ran over to her and kicked her hard in the thigh.

Thank God she managed to get some distance from that arsehole. And give mum her due, as she stood defiantly shouting at him and the rest of them, she made no attempt to re-adjust her clothes or her hair. I can clearly see her standing there now with blood running from both her knees and as she shook her hands at him there was blood on them too. Poor woman. I have spoken to her about that day and she tells me it was planned between my father and her that she could take us two kids out for the day on the bus to the town centre, whilst my father was at work in Luton. Apparently when she arrived the family had a suspicion that she was going to take us away for good.

That was never the case. She told me she wouldn't have been able to; with no car, no money and owing to her being partially disabled from polio in the lower legs. All she wanted was some time with her own children. She has never forgiven them for the unnecessary level of hostility they met her with that day. And neither have I.

Time in Rugby

Sometime after all this turmoil, my sister and I joined my father where he was living in Rugby. He was renting but it was the biggest house I had ever been inside. A four-bedroomed 1950's detached house, sitting on a corner plot with gardens all around. It had a massive garage with a set of heavy wooden doors that ran on rails when opened. At first he lived there on his own and his only company would be his secretary, whose name was Sheila. She was a very pretty lady, tall with long dark straight hair, maybe a slight wave to it. Blue eyes and a fine figure. She would come into the house from time to time and do her work. When we arrived on the scene not much seem to change for us, as my father was always at work and the new secretary would look after us.

One morning on my way to the bathroom I saw Sheila came out of Dad's bedroom in her nightdress, and I realised then that she was now sleeping with my father. Her two daughters had also moved in with us that same night and were sleeping in the smallest room at the rear of the house. What was nice about the relationship he was having with Sheila was that there was very little arguing or shouting that we knew about.

I remember one night he woke my sister and me up at around eleven o'clock in the evening. We were both very sleepy and tired, but we still had the surprise of our lives. When we went downstairs and into the living room we both just stood in the doorway looking in with astonishment He and Sheila had made a complete party scene complete with decorations, cakes, sausage rolls and jelly along with cheese sticks and sandwiches with different fillings. We slowly began to wake up and eat some tasty things and drink lemonade. At about midnight we could stay up no longer. Mr sandy man had returned. I feel he got much more out of this than we did, but we do have the memory of the event and maybe that's what he intended all along.

(The reason for this extravaganza was explained to me by Sheila, Your father had a personal wish to have his very own "Beano" (A *midnight party for no reason at all*) and now he's had one he is very pleased about it.)

I have no idea what work my father was doing at this time or how long the relationship with Sheila had been going on. Now my father has passed away I will never know what happened to them and why they parted. I was told from an unreliable source that she had gone back to her previous partner. From meeting her and sharing some good times with her and her daughters it did not seem fair that she had gone at all. Soon it was to be the same for my sister and me and not before time.

***

Marina and I were very glad to hear we would be leaving our father soon. He had started drinking heavily and he was having extremely bad headaches during the night, as well as suffering some kind of depression. Sometimes in the middle of the night he would tell me to get out of my bed and sit with him on the stairs whilst he would cry and rage in agony that his head was trying to explode. He would thump the walls and stairs with great force, though he never seemed to hurt himself. During these times I could do nothing but try to keep out of harm's way.

One autumn afternoon he must have been at his darkest hour. He collected Marina and I from our school playing field but he said nothing to us, he just made hand gestures. When we came through the gates he made no explanation of what was going on or why he was taking us out of school. He opened the rear car door and in we went. He drove off at a normal speed. I looked at Marina for some explanation and she just shrugged her little shoulders.

He didn't speak a word to us as we drove along out of Rugby in complete silence. After an hour or so he eventually pulled over, still saying nothing, just sat there looking out the front window. I was again looking to Marina and holding her hand discreetly so he wouldn't know we were scared of him.

The silence was disturbing enough, but seeing him just staring across the fields and lakes added to this, and he seemed full of a strange darkness. Then he lowered his head down and cupped it in both hands grumbling about his headache coming back, and started to softly cry. This was a terrible situation for me and Marina as he became inconsolable. We could do nothing but look at each other and every so often peer out of the windows hoping someone would walk by. Now our stomachs started feeling as though they would erupt any second. As I was looking out the window it suddenly dawned on me that we had been to this site before, this was the deepest of the brickwork lakes. (*Somewhere near Bedford, I now know*).

He and Sheila had brought us all here for a walk and told us all about the cranes that had been abandoned in the bottom of this very pit, and when the water came in and covered them all up they got stuck there. He told us that they were still down there in the deepest parts and nobody could now retrieve them. This must be a special place for him but it was nothing to us. In fact it was a very gloomy and a dark place to be in even in the summer, it had a strange and forlorn feel to it.

I was starting to feel more uncomfortable, Marina and I kept discreetly looking at each other and I started twitching my feet. Then he slowly began to raise his head, he then turned around and stared right through us both with an evil glare that would fit any horror movie. We didn't dare move or blink. Both Marina and I knew this was a really bad moment and that something was about to happen. We did not know what it was going to be but the atmosphere was thick and heavy with danger. This frozen moment in time seemed to last forever and I was thinking of making a run for it, but I didn't dare move a muscle. I am proud to say that at that moment I had a good grip on Marina's coat, and if something odd was to happen I was ready to pull her out with me; whether or not we would have got away is a story that thankfully has not to be told.

He broke down in some miserable blubbery mess. Shortly after, and to my extreme relief, he turned around and started the engine and slowly started to move away from this place. He drove us all the way home, still looking stressed. Looking back now I do believe he was considering the possibility of drowning us or something awful, maybe he lacked the courage or he realised the stupidity of his thoughts. Maybe he just went somewhere he enjoyed. I will never know and I'm glad to be able to forget all about it.

Right Town, Wrong Station

During our time in Rugby my mother would make contact with us via the phone. On one occasion she told us that she had moved to the Isle of Wight and settled in a little village called Gunville. She also told us that there was a magnificent castle just a little way up the hill from where she was now living, called Carisbrooke castle. She was living with a man called Frank in a semi-detached council house near the bottom of Gunville road and about four or five doors from the stream. Amazingly, a week later my sister and I found ourselves on an exciting train journey from London to Portsmouth to join her.

My father drove us from Rugby to a London railway station, and arranged for a fellow passenger, also travelling to Portsmouth, to keep an eye on us to our final destination. What a day our train journey was to be, and what a fantastic experience for me. Sitting at the window watching things pass by so fast and seeing all the different stations we stopped at during our journey. After an hour or so, we eventually arrived at Portsmouth railway station. The man who had looked after us told Marina and I that this was the station we had to get off. So without any fuss we followed the other passengers off and looked all about to see what would happen next. The man with us asked me what my mother looked like because there was nobody waiting at the platform for us. He thought she might be in the cafe. I wasn't sure what she looked like anymore so just explained she had black hair and was disabled in the legs. As he could not find her and had no contact number he took us to the station masters office and told them our plight, said goodbye and off he went.

The station master sat us down and asked me where we going to that day. I explained that we were to live with our mother on the Isle of Wight and that she was to collect us at the station and take us on a ferry. Just at that moment the loud whistle sounded and people outside on the platform hastened their movements.

The station master dashed out of his office door and made his way to the man with the whistle, who was holding a green flag. The station master spoke with this man for a few moments and then returned to us in the office where I was already standing in his office doorway watching all that was going on. He explained to me and my sister that we had got off at the wrong station. It was Portsmouth station, but it was the town station not the ferry station. So he rushed us out of his office and put us back onto the train in the same seats we had travelled in on the way down. Phew, that was a bit scary, I thought to myself.

Within ten minutes of the train leaving, we arrived at Portsmouth ferry station which was on steel supports that allowed the train to stop its journey out and over the sea. I could not believe I was looking at the blue sea beneath the train we had just come in on. This time my mother was there waiting for us with a big smile and arms open wide, I didn't understand why she was crying because we felt happy and excited. The station master had telephoned my mother whilst she was at the station to make sure she would wait for us on the platform. When she walked us to the ship it was almost too much excitement to take in. I kept looking back at the train station on the water and then at the sea and the ship again. It was a sight to match many experiences.

My mother standing on the platform waiting for us was an image lost in my memory for many years until it suddenly came back to me one winter's night when I arrived at Kettering station. This time, I was met on the platform by another beautiful lady emanating the same joyful smile as she welcomed me to her comforting embrace. She was just as pleased to see me as my mother had been forty five years earlier. Both scenes are now securely embedded into my mind and could easily have been part of any emotional movie.

My mother was going to take us both on the ferry for the first time and across the sea to get to her new life. We were going to have a new life with our mother and her new boyfriend Frank. She told us he had a nice house and an Alsatian dog called Vixen, but we didn't mind as long as we were away from Rugby.

My sister and I had never been on a ship or even a boat before, so when we walked towards the massive white passenger ferry it was very exciting. I noticed the vessel had a large brass horn fitted to the roof and I so wanted to hear it go off. When my mother gave the man our tickets he let us walk up the netted gantry onto the ship's deck. We walked across a sea of mahogany with such a deep shine to it you could see you own reflection. Some of the ship's doors were made from the same wood, while others were steel. I noticed that they all had large well-polished brass handles on them. It was fascinating to watch the water rush by as the ship was cutting through the sea making the gulls fly all around us calling out with their typical seaside call.

Frank

About an hour after leaving Portsmouth harbour we arrived at our destination, the Isle of Wight. We were aboard the foot passengers' ferry so we arrived at the head of the famous pier of Ryde. We walked off the ferry a few metres away and straight onto a little train that took us along the famous and very longer pier to the town, where Frank was waiting for us. This short train trip lasted at most ten minutes, which was very disappointing for me, as the sea could plainly be seen outside the train windows and on both sides. We were met by a very large man, much bigger than my father and he had a calming gentle smile. "Oh, brilliant," I said aloud, "he's got a car!" My sister and I moved in and settled down with mother and Frank, as you do, and it was nice to never once see them fight or hear them arguing. In fact I think they got on for the most part quite well.

My new school was lovely. Built in red brick, a Victorian design primary school and situated at the top of a hill. Discipline was very important at this school and seemed to be all around me. Once I saw a teacher threaten a young boy with a soapy mouth wash if he was to swear again whilst playing. You guessed it, we boys are pretty stupid. As I watched him playing I could tell he was winding up the same teacher and as sure as night becomes day, she grabbed him and pulled him over a basin that was nearby and did just what she threatened him she would do and used a real bar of soap. I never swore anyway and I had no intention to do so here, even I did outside of school.

It was in this playground where I had my first "self" awareness. It was a warm day with bright blue sky and during the lesson breaks we were all playing in the playground and running around like you do. As I was the new chap, I had not yet made any friends so played on my own. Some of the boys would run to the metal climbing frame in the playground and climb all over it 'till the bell rang. I was not yet confident enough to walk over and join them without an invitation, so I would hang around until the bell rang; when they got down and made their way inside I would quickly climb on and get as far up as I could before being told otherwise.

This day the teacher had not realised I was still outside on the frame and she went in and left me to my own devices. I was all alone in the playground and had this impressive climbing frame all to myself. With the sun shining on me what else could I have asked for, nothing, but I did receive something extra! Climbing up was fun, but I soon discovered the sliding down a warm pole tightly gripped between my legs sliding along my groin was a feeling I had never before experienced. I hastily re-climbed the frame as many times as I could to be able to enjoy the erotic downward slide. I would slide down so often and so slowly that it was starting to hurt me a little, so I rested halfway down. Whilst hanging there I looked across to my classroom and could see most the kids at the window watching me. (*Nice one!*)

***

This school had cross country lessons; to me nothing could be a worse. I could never keep up and I was always out of breath so would be the last one back every time. In fact I was so fed up with the whole thing; I would just sit down half way round and kill ants and bugs. Sometimes I would find a large flat stone and using another, would write my name on it and put it down till next time. The route we took was always the same, a figure of eight with the school in the middle. Good fortune had it that a public play area was adjacent to the school and hidden from view by some large broadleaf trees. I mastered the art of ducking out here on my way round and would openly play there until the class would go past, then I would take my time and just walk in behind them at my leisure. Nobody said anything. I learned then that I could have some control in my life, so I would always try to be me and not follow if I chose not to.

***

One winter's afternoon whilst at home with my mother and Frank, I was playing with my cars on the living room floor. There was a loud knock at the front door and my mother went to answer it. It turned out the young man at the door was Frank's eldest son of fourteen. He did not live with his father but would pop in every so often. I had never seen him before. His name was Kevin and he looked a bulky lad with mean eyes.

He was introduced to me and not long afterward was playing with me and my cars on the floor. Something happened during the game, I'm not sure what, but at one point he refused to give me back one of my cars. My mother intervened attempting to resolve the issue fairly, Frank told her to keep out of it and let us sort it out between ourselves. She reluctantly obeyed. Kevin, hearing that, thought he now had a licence from his father to bully me further and decided to punch me in the face and push me over onto my back enabling him to sit on my stomach and slap me a few times. Not satisfied that he had inflicted enough pain and humiliation upon me, he raised himself up a little and placed his knees into my eyes and knelt on them with all his weight. The discomfort and pain was all I could bear and try as I might to shift the chubby loaf off I could not budge him. My mother must have got up and pulled him off me for all of a sudden he was gone. My eyes were sore from the salt in my tears, which made things even worse.

As I walked home from school one afternoon, I could see in the distance a police car parked outside Frank's house. This was the first time I had seen one in our village, let alone outside Frank's house. I felt a little nervous because it reminded me of the troubled times we had in Deanshanger. I soon arrived at Frank's gate and made my way to the back door, as I went into the kitchen I could see two policemen standing by the sink talking to Frank and my mother. It all seemed a bit disturbing as the mood was tempered to sullen. My mother took me into the front room and told me she and Frank had to go to the hospital to see Kevin. My mother began explaining Kevin's misfortune to me. I found it difficult not to smile and felt blessed when I heard what he had done to himself. I was now able to enjoy the last laugh.

To my delight and pleasure, Frank's son, Kevin had been playing truant from his school and went up to the castle with his girlfriend. In an attempt to show off, he had informed her he reckoned he could get into the castle without paying the entrance fee by climbing an old tree close to the castle wall, climbing up and getting inside. She must have been impressed and maybe encouraged him to demonstrate this feat of daring behaviour.

He climbed the tree and reached the top where he could cross over and onto the wall, but (*luckily!*) he fell to the ground from such a height, and landed with such force, he broke both of his legs! God! I so hoped he was in agony. For quite a while after, I would go to bed and imagine I had been there and witnessed the event, thinking of having spent ages kicking his broken legs. A nasty thought I know, but delicious!

At the rear of Frank's house were several large fields, belonging to the local farmer. I would often play in these fields, chasing butterflies and dragonflies down by the stream. You could walk around them for miles and see nobody. A good distance from Frank's house was a derelict farm house which was always a favourite of mine. I used to pretend it was my house and I was the farmer, who could never get into the attic. (*Sad isn't it?*) Other times I would join Frank in mushroom picking, and I must admit with no exaggeration that I found the largest white mushroom ever found in Gunville. It was measured to be just less than twelve inches across the cap, as soon as we returned home Frank cooked it for us all to eat and it was bloody handsome!

The best way for me to enter these fields was by removing two or three spindles from the fence at the rear of Frank's garden that separated it from the field. At weekends and during summer months I would often walk off for hours at time and enjoy my own company amongst the other animals that may have been out there with me. I liked to play in some of the old ruined barns and would climb up into the rafters, or at other times would try climbing trees for a while and then move onto a lovely little brook that was some way over the far side. Here, I would paddle and then sit on the bank trying to spot fish or just watch butterflies and dragonflies.

I especially enjoyed swinging on a rope from a tree some older boys had attached to a thick branch way up high. Swinging was always fun until I cracked my knee on a root stump. I was often joined in the field with a large number of fully grown pigs and sometimes half grown cattle, called bullocks. They were harmless and never bothered me; we all got on just fine.

Some mornings before I went to school I would move the spindles and get into the fields, for I had a spiteful new game to play with the pigs. Behind one of the nearby hedges, the farmer had a dilapidated old brick pen full of big pink pigs and dozens of piglets. They would be walking about sniffing and snorting as they happily went on with their business. The brick walls were showing signs of age and many bricks had crumbled away, with debris scattered all about. I found it great fun to collect this material and make piles of it on top of the lowest wall surrounding the pigs. I would then throw and hurl it at the pigs, then the piglets. They would be screaming and running in a blinding panic, making a hell of a noise, but I loved it.

I had been making an object out of paper and cardboard for a while at school and on this particular day I was proudly taking it home to present to my mother. With a joy in my step and a smile on my face I was keen to get home. You can imagine the total shock and surprise I had when as I turned to corner of the house to go through the opened kitchen door, my mother suddenly appeared and slapped me twice in the face causing me to drop the paper and cardboard creation, and to use both my hands to shield me from more abuse. As she began shouting and ranting at me slowly the picture of my wrongdoing began to unfold.

That morning before going to school, I had been bullying the pigs again, and hadn't realised I was running late because I was so carried away with my cruel fun. When I did realise I was going to be late for school, I dashed out of the field through the fence and off to school, but I had forgotten to replace the three wooden spindles in Frank's wire fence.

Sometime later, and after I left for school my mother had put her washing on the washing line and went back into the house. A little later the pigs in the field behind Frank's house came strolling up the hedgerows and eventually made their way along the wooden fence at the rear of the houses. One pig found the gap I had left in Frank's fence. Once one pig had gone through, they all went through to Frank's garden and began eating Frank's plants and vegetables. They must have found my mother's washing very interesting because it was soon brought down to the ground and trampled all over. But worse was to follow, as my mother had left the back door open. While she was upstairs making the beds and vacuuming, a few of the pigs had entered the kitchen. My mother explained to me years later that when she was upstairs hoovering the bedrooms she could hear some odd noises coming from down stairs but had no idea what it was until she went down to the landing and looked down the stairs. It was then she saw a large pig at the bottom of the stairs looking up at her, for a moment she could not believe what she was looking at.

When the penny dropped, she flew into rage and ushered the pig out of the hallway only to find even more pigs in her kitchen. She could not kick them though she wanted to, so she grabbed the broom and chased them out, back into the garden. Knowing what my mother looks like when she's angry, if the pigs saw her rage they would have fought with themselves to get out without her having to lift a finger. Apparently when she chased them the pigs split into two groups. One group ran off up the garden whilst the other group turned left and through the open gate ran into the main street. My mother was unable to do much about it so she closed the front gate behind them and focused her attentions on getting the other pigs back through the fence.

It was at this moment she saw her clean washing all twisted and filthy on the ground. She then saw the mess and destruction the pigs had made to Frank's garden, and many of his vegetables eaten or destroyed. She managed to get the pigs out of the garden and back through the fence and into the field. My mother placed the missing spindles back in their rightful positions. She had no intention of doing anything regarding the pigs, who by now were walking up our street, and left them to fend for themselves. Later in the day she was asked if she knew anything about an incident when some escaped pigs got into the Sunday school chapel. She claimed no knowledge of it and confirmed our innocence to all who would ask.

When Frank came home my mother played down the incident, but he had already been told by the farmer who had been looking to see where his pigs had got out. When he looked over at our fence he could clearly see the mess his pigs had made along with the muddy foot prints leading down our path along the side of the house and out to the front gate. I saw another side to Frank that evening!

Vixen

Frank's dog, an Alsatian called Vixen, lived in a larger than normal sized kennel outside in the back yard. One time she had a litter of ten pups. As pups go, they were lovely enough but unfortunately got me into a lot of bother. To Frank the puppies were a cash crop for money that was needed. When the pups were a few days old, Frank asked me to keep an eye on them in the kennel, whilst he and my mother went shopping. It was my responsibility to make sure Vixen had plenty of water as she kept knocking her bowl over. I also had to make sure that no pups had been trapped behind her in the kennel as they could be killed if not rescued in time. This task was quite a responsibility as vixen was very protective of her pups and I was scared to move her if she was laying on one. After a while I became bored sitting around popping in and out to check on the pups, so I went off up the lane for a walk and to find other stuff to do.

On my return, and to my horror, my mother and Frank had already returned back at the house. They had an expression on their faces that indicated I was in big trouble. Leaving the dog and her pups had proved a step too far. I began to explain in a convincing manner, that I had just popped out for a couple of minutes to see one of my friends just a few doors up the street.

My effort, though courageous, proved to be pointless and as Frank looked across the kitchen at me he pointed at the draining board where two of Vixen's puppies lay dead. He had placed them both neatly down onto some newspaper. Oops! Or more like "Oh shit," I thought "Yes!" Frank shouted at me, "They're dead, and whose fault is that?"

I wanted to say "it's your damn dog's fault" but no way would I dare! He gave me the third degree, demanding to know exactly where had I been and for how long they had been left alone, like that was going to change things! When he eventfully pulled his face out of mine and stood back a little, he summoned me to the draining board and told me it was going to be my job to wrap the dead puppies in the newspaper they were laying on and then some more before throwing them in the dustbin.

His punishment now moved onto the next level. I was ordered to take my shoes and socks off then my shirt and was then marched to the kennel. He made me get into the kennel and sit on the floor with the puppies and Vixen until he returned to let me out again. He then closed and locked the door on me.

There was just enough light coming through gaps and splits in the wooden panels enabling me to see the dog and her puppies as they laid there. Because the puppies were all black, it was quite difficult to distinguish one from the other and what was going on every time they moved. During my time in the kennel nothing undue happened to the pups or the dog, thank goodness. After a few hours he came back to let me out and gave me another lecture on my irresponsible attitude, though I was only seven! To this day I cannot stand the smell of new born puppies or the thought of living in a kennel!

***

The boys in the village were quite tough, and no matter how hard I tried to be a part of their gang I was always the new boy to them so nobody called at my door for me to join with them in their adventures.

One afternoon, I was walking Frank's dog up the village lane when I came across several boxes of tomatoes either abandoned or dumped in the ditch on the side. This could be a good find, I reckoned and I felt I should give them to my mother. I dropped down into the ditch and picked a couple up to have a closer look.

Unfortunately they must have been rotten or going rotten, for they were soft and going black. Who dumped them there and why, I had no idea, but they had gone out of their way to bother taking them up the lane.

I walked about half a mile or so keeping Vixen on the lead all the time, taking my time. When I reached the top of the lane I'd had enough so we turned round and made our way back towards home. About halfway through our return journey I could see through odd gaps in the trees, the local gang coming up the hill towards me. I was a little concerned because they had long sticks and were looking rather boisterous. In my mind I needed to come up with something to catch their attention so we could stop and talk or something in an attempt to become friends.

I came up with what I thought was a brilliant idea; I ran over to the hedge row and pulled off a long thin branch from the nearest bush. I then dipped the tip into one of the many mud filled puddles in the lane. I began using it like Japanese's paint brush I drew long muddy lines on Vixens back making it look as if I had been beating her. This clever act would show the gang I was a tough new kid in the village and a careless dog beater with no fear so they should take heed.

Regrettably my plan had a potential flaw; it could look like I was a cruel spiteful young boy who enjoyed picking on a defenceless dog. The boys came closer and closer till they saw me and vixen. They quickly made their way over to me and gathered all around. The boys were looking at me first then vixen, shuffling around for better positions to begin studying the harsh injuries I had inflicted on this nice looking dog. I held my position with my back straight and my head held proud with my whipping stick still grasped tightly in my right hand.

The biggest boy stared at me then he asked "did you do that"? I looked him back and straight into his eyes, "Yes, she's been trying to get away" I explained making my forehead frown with as I looked at vixen with disapproval. "Well that's bloody cruel you sad sod" he replied. Then all the boys seemed to unite together in anger with a look of vengeance on their faces as they surrounded me. I sensed I could now be in deep trouble and there was not an adult anywhere in sight to pluck me out of harm's way. I looked for a gap in the crowd of angry boys, but without any warning my nerve broke and I just ran for it as fast as my terrified legs could carry me. They chased me for a while but to my utter relief they slowed down and I made good my escape.

At the bottom of the lane I washed off the fake whipping lines I had made on vixens back. The last thing I wanted was an adult to see the marks and tell Frank! With the dog clean and shiny again, I made my way along the street to home. As I entered the house I put a big smile on my face and told my mother we had enjoyed our walk and had found some tomatoes in the ditch, but that I had to leave them because they had gone rotten.

That evening we had our dinner as usual around six o'clock and afterwards went into the living room to watch the TV. Not long after we had settled down, the back door knocked and my mother went to see who it was. When she came back into the living room she told me that it was the lads from the village who were all at the back door wanting to see me. She questioned me on what had I been up to. I assured her I had done nothing wrong at all.

"Well," she said, "that's funny; because they've told me they wish to be friends with you again and say sorry to you. So what's that all about?" She asked me again. I assured her it was nothing. I quickly made my way to the back door to see what they wanted. I made sure I closed the living room door behind me just in case. How odd, I thought, what on earth could they be up to?

I arrived at the back door looking a little nervous and said hello to the gang of boys outside. Some of the younger boys were giggling while the others looked more intensely at me. The tallest boy leaned forward and said quietly, "Sorry about making you run away earlier, we have brought you something." And at that precise moment everybody outside hurled rotten tomatoes at me, at least a dozen or more, right into my mother's kitchen.

I instantly reacted by ducking down and catching only a couple on my clothes, but the rest splattered all over the kitchen. Some hit the table, some the walls. The ones that hit the walls made an enormous mess because they exploded on impact, and bits of bright red tomato had covered a massive amount of wall, some splattering so hard they plastered the ceiling as well. I looked around in disbelief. Oh my God! I thought what a bloody great mess. When my mother heard the noise and commotion from the kitchen she became suspicious and came through to have a look at what was happening. She had seen the boys running fast out the front gate and up the street; she knew something had kicked off.

As she came in to see what was up, her eyes popped out of her head and her bottom jaw just dropped open. She was swearing at me and looking all around at the same time, Heavens alive, she murmured over and over again. We both had a massive task ahead of us so we set to and cleaned every last trace before Frank could get involved.

***

A little time after the tomato incident I regained my confidence and took Vixen for a long walk up the same lane again. I had made a new friend whose name escapes me now. When I told him about the lane and all the interesting things I had found and experienced walking there, he decided to come along and join in some of my adventures. To make things a little more interesting that morning, I had stolen Kevin's catapult from under his bed and I thought we could have some fun with it and impress my new friend at the same time.

We set off and were soon walking along the lane. I would find suitable stones to fire from the catapult and would allow my new friend the odd go for himself. In the main I had the prized catapult and this made me feel good and important. I decided to make a detour and took a path through the hedge so we could get to a rookery that was well known to the local boys and now me.

As my friend and I walked through the fields I would tease him by picking up large pieces of dry cow dung and throwing it at him. As we got near to the crows we could clearly see them flying high in the sky around making their crow noises aloud. I told my friend the crows were not happy we were so close to them and the rookery and that's why they were trying to scare us off. With all the noise and commotion they were making they nearly succeeded. I decided to walk with the dog directly beneath the same trees the crows were sitting in so I could have a pop at them with the catapult. This was a good idea, so that's what we set out to do. We fired many stones at the crows and missed every single one we aimed at. Or so we thought. As we came to the end of the rookery I became fed up with walking and missing so many birds, that I suggested we to go back following the route we had come along.

As we returned beneath and along the rookery, I saw an injured crow hopping around in the field ahead of us. It was obvious it had suffered an injury to its right wing. It could have been a result of a stone from the catapult fired by us. It was possible the stone had struck the bird without either of us knowing. Or it could have happened elsewhere. Whatever the reason, my killing intent had left me and I was now feeling very guilty and full of remorse. I felt it was my duty to help this poor thing and so I convinced my friend to help me catch it before it could get away or harm itself even more.

We moved slowly around it, encircling it with the dog as well! The injured crow tried to out-smart us every time. I had the idea of tying our two jumpers together by the sleeves and throwing the jumpers over it; this was worth a try so we took off our jumpers and tried out my idea to good effect.

After several attempts we were successful and we caught the injured crow. We both ran over to the trapped crow and I gently picked it up from underneath our jumpers. It was shouting at me as its glassed black eyes stared at me. I held the crow firmly in my hands and began to study it closely. I had never held a crow before and this became a special moment for me. I now felt terrible that my friend or I may have been the culprits of this bird's suffering, and quietly promised to myself that I would never hurt a bird again. With hindsight, it proved a promise I would not keep.

The responsibility I had of keeping Vixen safe, and on her lead was transferred from me to my friend as I wanted to take charge and care for the injured crow. I made it as comfortable as I could by placing it into one of the jumpers and then holding it between my hands to keep its wings closed. This allowed it to see where it was going. With my valuable feathered friend safely within my hands, we set off back home. I took care to hide the catapult from sight, by pushing it far down into my underpants.

I explained to my friend the dangers of meeting the local gang on this lane and what they would do if they thought we had done harm to the crow I was carrying. This information made my friend nervous and I could clearly see his complexion and facial expression change from the excitement we had been enjoying to a fear from the possibility of being harmed by a gang of older boys. (*Poor little chap*)

We all made it safely back to the lane and down to the road without meeting a soul. As we walked down the main road on the way to my house, several younger children ran up to me to see the majestic and shiny black crow I was looking after with great care and pride. It was not long before the bigger boys heard of my bird and one or two of them asked me if they could see it more closely and another asked if he could have it for a pet. Nobody could offer me anything that was enough for me to give up my prized possession. I was going to have the crow as a pet and that was that. When we arrived home I was going to ask Frank if he would show me how to help the crow to recover from its injury with the intention of letting it go again. Unfortunately, Frank was away that weekend so I had to wait until his return

By the time we reached my house we had a little gathering around us making us look and feel special. When my mother met us both at the kitchen door she clearly had different ideas as to my new found popularity, and she showed no compassion for the crow either. "You can get rid of that thing," was her attitude. I explained to her it was my intention to help the crow recover and let it go. I thought that by the time the crow had recovered my mother would have become used to it and allow me to keep it.

To my surprise and great pleasure my mother came down the garden path towards me carrying a large cardboard box. She had made some holes all around it and informed me this would be a good way of keeping the crow in one place so I could help it get better, but I had to keep the bird in the shed and not bring it into the house. This I readily agreed to, as my mother had been kind to offer her help given her previous experience of birds in her kitchen!

My friend gave me a wave as he made his way out the front gate, and I went into the shed to see my crow again. My mother told me the crow would appreciate some worms to eat so I should dig a few up for him.

I found one of Frank's garden forks and started to dig for worms in a patch of turned soil. Funny how when you want worms there seems to be none yet other times they're everywhere. This went on for several days and I became quite attached to my crow. At school I would tell the teachers all about it and would draw it during drawing lessons and keep other children up to date with its progress. The crow had helped me to become popular and accepted within the school and that's the best thing it could have ever done for me.

After school one day I went home as usual and did the things you do when you first get in. I grabbed a couple of biscuits and a quick sandwich, and chased it down with a glass of orange squash. This day was going to be a little different for me. My mother was happy for me to go off to the shed for some time where my crow was living without changing from my school clothes before I had to do any homework. Today I had planned to let the crow out of his box to get some sunlight.

As I made my way past the shed window to the shed door I could see the box that had the crow inside was already open. That doesn't look good, I thought, this means the crow has got out and is maybe strong enough to lift the lid, and has tried to make his escape. I might have a problem now in keeping him in the shed while I enter through the door. I carefully and slowly opened up the door and closed it behind me. I stood still for a moment while I listened for him moving about inside, but there was no sound at all.

I realised the crow had gone! I went to my mother and told her about the empty box and the crow's disappearance, but she knew nothing about it, so she asked Frank if he knew anything. Frank replied he had a visit from his son Kevin that day and had told him about the crow and said I should go and ask him about it.

I was not happy at all about the information that Kevin had been over and been in the shed with my pet crow. I had a tear in my eye as I ran out the gate in search of him. My tears were part rage and part sadness; I hated him for taking my pet and I didn't know what he was doing with it.

I soon found Kevin up the playing fields with some of his friends. I ran straight up to him crying and shouted "Where is my crow, you bastard?" he pushed me away laughing and invited me to come at him again. I duly obliged, and with much more force this time. It made no difference however and he grabbed me by the neck and whilst still laughing told me he had swapped the crow with one of his mates for a penknife and then pushed me away again. He turned his back on me and carried on as if I wasn't there.

He had no right to do that, and I was enraged and gutted at the same time. I ran out of the park and back down the road to find which of his mates had the crow, as Kevin wouldn't tell me.

Nobody seemed to be about, so I had to look around the sides of his friends' houses that I knew off. As my pace started to slow down, sadness started to take over my feeling of anger. I now walked along the road looking for clues. I kept thinking about my crow, trying to remain confident that I would eventually find it. When I walked past the Sunday school chapel, I saw the large wooden gate at the side of the building next door open. I was suspicious, and had a feeling this was odd as the building next to the chapel had been abandoned and been locked up for some time. We used to say it was haunted, so nobody dared try to get into it or over the walls into the gardens. How come the gate was now open? I quietly crept along the side path and peered through the opening.

To my horror and bitter disappointment I saw my lovely shiny black crow tied to an old washing line. It was dead. I went across to have a better look at it and I could see clearly it had been shot many times by an air gun. I stood still right in front of it and looked at all the broken feathers and the blood matted in-between them. Its majestic head was a mess, and its beak was open with its narrow thin dry tongue pointing out as stiff as a pencil. I stepped back a few feet and sat on a pile of rubble just looking at the crow. My mind took me back in time a few days, and I could see my friend and I having a great time walking along the rookery and watching the crows flying in the clear skies. I felt ashamed of what I had done that day firing at the crows. I felt I was ultimately responsible for the crows end.

I got up and walked away at a normal pace, taking a last glance at it as I passed through the gate for the last time. I deliberately left it hanging on the clothes line, for I wanted nothing more to do with the poor thing. On my arrival home I met my mother in the front garden but made no song and dance about it. I just told my mother what I had found and what had happened and that was that. A few weeks later I did have a chance to see Kevin's new penknife and could have pinched it if I wanted, but I didn't as I still had his catapult hidden in the shed. Not many weeks later I heard he had lost it the stream when he and his mates went night fishing.

Christmas

Christmas was fast approaching, and the ground seemed constantly wet and the air always cold. My mother had put the Christmas decorations up and the excitement of the twenty-fifth's arrival was always in our hearts and minds. That Christmas Eve my mother, who was catholic, wanted us to join her and a couple of friends at the midnight mass, held in the church of Gunville. Just like a Charles Dickens story, the day of the twenty-forth was a picture of white snow. The church was a few miles by road and with the roads impassable due to the heavy snow we had to walk. The best way for us to get there was to cut across the fields at the back of our houses. And this is what everybody in our village who was going did. The evening became dark and the snow had stopped. Mother told us to get ready and we prepared ourselves for walking across the snow covered fields to take the short cut to the church about a mile away.

The first part of our journey was on the pavement towards the field gate at the top of the village. There were a few street lights along the road, making the snow look orange and warm. We walked past my Sunday school and then past the local store. Soon afterwards we reached the gate we had to go through to go cross-country.

As we made our way across the field we were in total darkness, with only the brightness of the moon shining on the snow to enable the adults to see where we were going. It wasn't long before the snow was making our feet wet and cold. We went past the rear of a large factory that had been deserted many years ago and onto the barren wasteland. Now it seemed to Marina and I that we had no landmarks to guide us all along, and the walk seemed to go on for ages. Eventually we could see a warm orange light shining through the dark trees, surrounding our side of the churchyard. We could also see people standing beneath the dimly lit lantern hanging from an arch above the church gates. We eventually arrived at the gates and made our way along the path and into the church. My mother made a big fuss and bother to the church warden and insisted we be allowed to sit upstairs in the pews so she could see and participate in the evening's service. Otherwise with her being so short she would have witnessed nothing.

The service commenced around eleven-thirty or so, and went on a bit, as they seem to for youngsters. Eventually the preaching and singing stopped and the priest downstairs at the front of the church asked all those who wanted to drink the blood of Christ and eat a small circle of bread should come forth. I was startled that anybody would want to drink a man's blood, but I could eat a slice of bread. I asked my mother if I was allowed down to receive some. She was not happy at all that I could be so disrespectful in God's house, and cuffed me over the head, making me sit with Marina until she came back. I watched her move slowly along the queue downstairs and arrive at the priest. By the time my mother had her blood and bread the queue was very short, so I seized my opportunity to run downstairs to try the circle of bread.

She saw me but couldn't get to me when I was in the front, and so allowed me to continue. She waited for me to come past the man holding the silver cup of blood and smiled at me as she took my hand and escorted me back upstairs. Soon it was all over and we had to make our way home. When we got outside it was a sight to behold, the dark night sky had disappeared and it was a wall of falling snow with such large flakes I have never seen since. Everybody was amazed at the change and all were talking about it as they moved along.

The church lights made the scene look as though we were walking through a Christmas card, it was all very surreal. When we passed the church gates and began our long walk home across the fields, we realised the footprints we had made in the snow as we arrived had now disappeared under four inches of fresh snow. The walk home will stay with me till the curtains on me fall. This was truly a memorable experience for all those who attended that wonderful night.

Caravans and Adventure

She had fallen in love with Frank, her second love, but in the end it proved to be a sad year for her. By the end of spring that year we were on the move again, this time to live in a static caravan, the sort you see in sites in places such as "Wells-Next-to-Sea". Only ours was the oldest and green with mildew and a collection moss over it. This was because it was pitched next to the trees and was already quite old when my mother took it on. A few years later I asked my mother about these times and she told me Cupids arrows of love fell short on her yet again, for my poor mother had to move out. Apparently Frank told her he wanted his own space and freedom again, although he claimed he still loved her. He also said he found two young children very restrictive and demanding.

My mother told me she kept in touch with her friends in Gunville, and for a time they would keep her informed as to what was going on with Frank and any other village gossip. They told her Frank's wife had come back into his life and was living with him again. My mother must have been devastated, though I never saw her down about it, not once. Several years later she met Tony, who lived in Portsmouth, and he was her third and lasting love. She is still with Tony to this day. She tells me he can be a pain in the arse but she would rather be together with someone who cares and adores her, than to try and find another man who could be passing through her life again.

The caravan site we now lived on was near to the car ferry terminal, just off East Cowes and on the corner of the main road leading east to Binstead, or west to West Cowes. Next to the caravan site was an orchard full of apple trees, plum trees with a few pear trees for good measure. My sister would come with me on scrumping missions. We didn't know it then, but we would soon see the owner coming for us waving a stick like a sketch from a children's story

66

book. We did in fact get away from him and had to abandon a basket full of pears that got stuck in the hedge as we made our escape. When the orchard owner came around the caravan site and knocked on our caravan door, my mother had to talk with him outside as already I had a vast collection of pears laid out on the bench seats and on the table from a previous daytime raid!

We also had no idea that in a few months' time the police would be talking to my mother about a young boy seen playing in the site compound that contained a large number of big red gas bottles. Somehow all the tops had been opened, and all the gas taps turned on, releasing the highly dangerous and flammable gas from all the cylinders into the site. Why knock on our door? Never did find out who the boy was.

***

It was from this humble little site that I really began to enjoy my life to the full, and as the next few passages will describe it was without any doubt the best life of young adventures a boy could dream of. Best I describe our new school in Binstead. Again it was of Victorian design and construction, red brick and buff coloured York stone window frames. It had two high pitched slatted roofs and a large brick entrance.

The school and the playground were about a metre lower than the path and roads around the school, and the top end of the playground about two metres lower than that. The top end was where, every so often, the coke for the boilers would be tipped into the playground from sacks that the men would pull from lorries.

I really enjoyed this school at first, but again I found myself isolated from the other children as I was the new boy, and taller than most. I used to try to join in with their games, but no one realised I didn't know the rules or how to play, so I would watch in an attempt to find out.

I was most vulnerable to bullying when I was not participating in playground games. As I was tall for my year I would stand out easily when doing nothing. The older boys would often see me as an easy target for them to pick on, to show how tough and important they were to their friends. It was just bullying, really, and I was sick of it. Depending on which one of the older boys was making his way over to me, I could more or less tell what was likely to be said or happen to me. Embarrassingly, on several occasions the girls in the playground would tell the older boys to "leave him alone"

One morning a lad came through the school gate into the playground carrying a long grass snake in his hands. He was showing it to everyone and was quickly surrounded by boys and girls of all ages. I was unable to see the snake and one of the girls told the boy with the snake "let him see it" and to my pleasure he did. After she had helped me I would often look for her and would really appreciate it when she walked around the playground with me

However, the constant intimidation was becoming a drag so I decided to have a break from it of my own accord. It was time for my own private outing.

My first day of truanting was only a half day, really. I decided to get out of school by myself after the break time following our daily bottle of milk. It's amazing to think we used to drink half a pint of milk every day at school around ten-thirty in the morning. Each day, a different milk monitor was selected by the teacher and he or she would have to take little milk bottles from the crates stacked up in the hallway and place one on each desk along with a wax straw. We would drink the milk in a given time and then we would have to cross our arms on top of our desks and lay our heads down on them for a little sleep. How quiet was that!

This was going to be my very own adventure time because I was going out. During the next playtime, I looked across at the closed school gate and without a moment's hesitation walked across to it and turned the iron latch up, allowing the gate to swing out into the playground. I walked through the gateway as bold as brass, up the step and onto the pavement. Nobody had noticed me going out, so I kept walking until I was out of sight. Not far from school was a grassy path leading to a small wooded area where the grass snake was found earlier in the same week. I was thinking maybe I could catch one for myself. That would be something, if I did, I proudly thought to myself.

The deeper I walked into the woods the darker it became. This proved a little intimidating for me, so after a brief visit I made my way out and back the way I had come. I had to walk past the school, but as it was lower than the road I couldn't be seen anyway. Not far from the school along the side road leading to the main street was a bakery and a Mr Kipling's cake shop. The cake shop had a side door which was usually open. I would pass by the bakery on my way to school every morning and if the side door was open I would often see many boxes of cakes and men moving them around.

As I walked by this time the door was open, and I could smell baking coming from inside. I walked to the door and curiously peered in. A man in a long white smock saw me as he walked past and asked if he could help me. I cheekily asked him if there were any broken cakes I could have. I knew I had a chance if I mentioned broken cakes, as my mother was getting broken biscuits from somewhere and I was sure she didn't pay for them. The man took a liking to my cheek and told me to "wait there son, I'll see what I've got for you" and that was the start of my friendship with the baker who supplied me with out of date cakes. I would have eaten most of them before

I arrived where I was going and other times I was given so many I was sick of them and would throw them about.

My favourite place to go was the sea and a lovely beach, about a twenty minute walk away. My first obstacle was a scary one for I had to cross the busy high street. When I was safely across I was able to disappear down Pitts lane and be safe from view because of a tall hedge.From then on, it was plain sailing as I would walk casually on my way to the church that I had to pass on my route. Finally I would have the delight of walking through a tree lined pathway where the trees were so tall they covered the lane, making a tunnel all the way down to the sandy beach. Once here, I had the sea and beach all to myself and if I met holiday makers there nobody said anything to me.

The more often I came to this beach, the less scared I became of the old church. Later I would walk around the churchyard and study the gravestones, reading them for something to do; I even went inside the church once when it started to rain so I could eat my cakes in some comfort. That is if you can call a wooden church pew comfortable.

My experience in the churchyard was a good grounding for me, because it helped me to overcome some fears I had about people dying and all that sort of stuff. On one of my latter outings I went with cakes in hand in the opposite direction, and ended up sitting on a sheet of corrugated steel in a different graveyard directly opposite the school I had just walked out. My legs dangling in an open grave must have been a sight to those passing by.

When telling people this story in the past I would say the two grave diggers where sitting with me but that was not accurate, they were sitting in their van smoking like chimneys. I was offered a puff on a cigarette but I didn't want it. I did offer them one of my cakes and they eagerly took it. When they finished I went to make a move, for it was not a good idea to be looking at your school from across the road when I should have been in it. Well the grave digging men seemed like decent chaps and I said good bye to them. At this point the driver's mate on the other side said "just a minute, son," and the bastard took me back to school.

(*So I say, never trust a grave digger!*)

The teachers had developed a system to keep an eye on me during play times. They had a ring of children who had agreed to tell the teachers if they knew I was going to go off again, and they had some older children who would chase after me when I made my runs to the school gate. They nearly always caught me. Once I made a dash for it and I could see people watching me. Up went the shout through the air in the playground, "Stop him!" I could see I was not going to make it to the gate this time as a large boy was already standing there smiling and waiting for his chance to grab me.

I looked all around me for a way out, and then I saw it. The coke for the boilers had been delivered and it had been poured over the wall as before, but was so deep it was just a few inches from the top of the school wall. I made a dash for if and ran straight up the face of this mountainous pile of coke. As I ran and climbed the children chasing me fell back one by one, as none of them would climb the enormous pile of coke. The success of my escape was far from certain, for as I mounted the top of the wall I saw the big boy who was at the gate blocking my escape just a few moments earlier. He had been told to run out of the school gate and catch me while I was on the wall. With one last effort I managed to climb up and over it just in time and ran down the road with this big kid after me. As I ran down the side road I saw the baker in his doorway having a cigarette. I waved at him as I ran by and he waved back looking very puzzled.

I did once manage to persuade my sister to join me on one of my outings, but that almost turned into a disaster threatening both of our lives. Somehow, we were both out of school and making our way down the side road. I wanted to show Marina the beach where I had played several times before. We quick stepped our way down what was now a familiar route to me. When we arrived at the beach the tide seemed quite a way out enabling us to play further away from the shore line. We walked for ages, and after some time realised the tide was slowly coming back in. As we made our way back we were drawing pictures in the sand with long sticks we had found earlier in the day. I was using my stick to move the rocks we found in the few rock pools around.

In one pool I was busy pulling out stones and larger rocks when a bright yellow snake slithered out and away from me and made its way to the incoming waves. I had never seen anything like it before so I chased it in attempt to catch it with my stick, but it sped off far too fast for me to get hold of it. I searched the rest of the pool just in case there was another in there but there was nothing else. I desperately looked around for another rock pool and could see some over in the distance, however I was not sure if we could get to it and back before the tide came. This would prevent us returning to the spot where we entered the beach. I gave it some thought and looked at the shore line to check that if I got the timing wrong could we still get out safely and off the beach. I reckoned we could do it, and a yellow snake would be worth the risk. If I found one and caught it, what a prize. (*Well, they say a man who hasn't made a mistake hasn't done anything!*)

Off we ran splashing through the water to the distant rock pools. By the time we got to them the tide had already covered the sand around them as well and I was starting to doubt my judgement in going.

Marina had every faith in me, and everything I did in her eyes was exciting and great fun, bless her! I had decided to make our search in this pool a quick one due to the water still rising all around us. I looked along the beach and al I saw was water. The sand had disappeared beneath, oh god, I thought. I'm starting to feel a little scared. I decided Marina and I should waste no more time here so I held her hand as we set off in the direction we had come onto the beach further down the coast. As I looked in the distance I could tell we couldn't make it back that way for the tide was coming in much faster now.

It looked better if we made our way straight back to the steep mud banks in front of us then follow them to find a way off the flooding beach. With no time to explain my increasing anxiety I shouted to Marina "Come on we've got to leg it!" When we reached the edge of the steep bank I had not realised we had been truly cut off from our desired route back to safety. In fact we had run into a cove, and though the tide was not fully in, we were trapped there. We couldn't get out of this bloody cove either because each side of it had already been buried under several feet of water.

Where we were standing the sand was now covered also. I looked up at the steep muddy cliff rising in front of us. They looked incredibly high, about twenty metres, and at the same angle as a house roof. We both ran through the sea water to the other side of the cove just in case we had a better chance there, but it was just the same. The water we stood in was now over our shoes and I was starting to realise the only way for us to go was up the steep mud bank in front of us or we would drown here.

Without wasting any more time I helped Marina up on the first part of the sticky mud and helped her to move on and up as quickly as she could. It was then we hit a massive problem; the mud was not mud at all, but very soft clay. No sooner had you placed your foot onto the surface it would sink in up to and past your ankles. This was funny for the first step but when you went to pull your foot out again it would not budge one millimetre. We were in a tight spot now, and facing a terrible predicament because we were stuck at the bottom of the mud cliff and the tide was fast rising up the cliff-face. On top of that, if I couldn't get us out of here nobody knew where we were to help us. What a disaster, I thought.

I stood still for a moment. Well, I had no choice actually. Our feet were still stuck. If we pulled too hard we could feel our shoes coming off in the mud so we had stopped pulling. To hell with our shoes, I said. I leant over to Marina and helped pull her feet out of the mud, leaving her shoes behind and then I did the same. It was bloody hard work climbing up that muddy cliff, and at times we had to lie on our tummies to stop us sinking too deep. But we made it and reached the pine forest. We cleaned ourselves the best we could and made our way home barefoot and looking like a couple of air raid survivors. There is no need to describe the welcome I received.

After this experience the school had a meeting with my mother in our caravan, with Marina and I present. It was agreed that a teacher would collect us both in the mornings, and take us home at the end of school, and that's what happened. I was also obliged to keep away from the sea unless I was with an adult.

Nature, Human and Otherwise

My out of school activities were now confined to the weekends in the main, and were definitely more inland. On one of my many walks across the field near where we lived in the caravan, I found all manner of things in one field. Buried amongst a mass of tall green stinging nettles and entwined with other flowers was a red tractor. It had no cab or attachments on the front or rear, and had no bonnet. I was abandoned to its resting place in the hedgerow. It still had its four wheels on and a black steering wheel, and a metal seat and two head lamps with the glass lenses still attached.

I tried to get to the driver's seat so I could sit on it but it proved totally impossible. I couldn't even get close to the seat, let alone sit on it. The thick nettles and the sharp brambles proved unforgiving and had cut me everywhere. If you could see this picturesque scene, you would most probably photograph it to share with others. If you had the mind to, you may even fantasize yourself refurbishing the tractor and bringing it back to its former glory. I could mislead you now and say I, too, wanted to polish it up and stuff. But that would not be in the true spirit of my history. No, I'm afraid to admit it, but I wanted to smash it to bits, especially the headlamps.

When I arrived home I told Marina about the walk, and what I had discovered in the hedge, and she was keen to see it for herself. She made me promise to take her and her friend there the next day. The next morning I was ready to go but Marina's friend was not so early (*girls!*). Finally, she turned up and was keen to join me in my walk. I was very pleased to get going, for it felt like I had been ready and waiting for ages. It was, I am sure, a precursor for my future adult life in waiting for the gentler sex to be ready at an agreed time (*It's just not going to happen!*).

We eagerly set off on our journey in the direction of the red abandoned tractor. I had given them long sticks for bashing stuff about, not understanding that girls don't bash stuff about! I had not told them I was intending to smash up the tractor but when I started to walk with a pick axe on my shoulder, questions were asked. I explained I was taking it back to where I had found it. This was not true (*shame on me*); the truth was I had found it much earlier in the compound with the gas bottles (*oops*). My reasons for taking it with me were twofold, one to smash and wreck the tractor and the other to impress the girls of my manliness. Unfortunately this was shortly to backfire on me.

We all walked for some time through a lovely golden countryside; the corn was ripe and the hedgerow flowers and insect life teeming with activity. We climbed over closed gates, stone walls and even fences. Some were made of wood, whilst others were wire. At about three quarters of the way into our journey we came to a public footpath and on one part of the path was a cross over stile. I went over first and Marina was close behind me, in fact she was too close behind me, for when I was crossing the stile I just had to show off to the girls, and made use of the pick axe to what I thought would be of great effect. I greatly underestimated the weight of it and made a big fuss of swinging it over my right shoulder.

Unfortunately I did not appreciate the combined weight and momentum of the pick axe as it swung through the air so it moved much further behind and away from my back and shoulder than I was expecting. I could sense Marina was behind me and that the pickaxe was on its way towards her. I couldn't do anything but allow it to travel the radius it was following. I turned at the same time as it came down and saw it graze Marina's nose and saw the blood that was appearing. Thank god the spike of the pick had missed her. It had been the metal collar on the end of the wooden handle that caught her and grazed her nose. Luckily the wound was just a light graze, and after a few minutes we started back on our way. That was far too close for comfort for me. I decided to throw the pickaxe into the hedge to get rid of it then and there. As a consequence the tractor survived our visit and remained intact, just as I had discovered it.

* * *

My father came over to visit us in the caravan one weekend. I was not comfortable with him coming to see us. The three of us had been getting on very well without his strict and overbearing ways. I can recall several things about his visit. One was him saying he was going to get me a model boat for me to float in the pond. And a four inch hunting knife complete with sheath, to take out on my adventures on the shore and in the woods. I have no idea what he promised Marina, but he said he would post it all to my mother on his return to the mainland. I thought he would be with us for the whole day and would then disappear again. I wouldn't have been bothered if he hadn't turned up at all.

Mother made dinner that evening and my father was there too. When it was time for Marina and I to go to bed he was still there. For the first time my mother put Marina and me in the top bed and pulled the partitions across separating us from them. I thought she did this so we would not be disturbed while they sat talking all night. During that evening, when Marina and I were in the end bed with the partitions closed, we tried to listen to what they were talking about, and this was exciting for us. A little later it seemed to go quiet and then I started to hear some soft noises and whispering. I was intrigued enough to stand on my bed and pull myself up so I could see over the top of the partitioning wall.

I could see my father laying on top of my mother and moving back and forth. I knew what he was doing alright; he was making love to my mother. I deliberately started to giggle in an attempt to put him off for I was confused and felt the urge to interfere. He was quite cross with me about this and turned around. Looking up at me he saw me peering over and started shouting at me to go back to bed and to get off the partitioning at once. I did as I was told but was feeling angry towards him and my mother for letting him use her like that. I was seven at the time and didn't understand my mother's needs! In the morning he left as quickly as he had arrived.

Our stay in the caravan was shortly to come to an end, and one Saturday morning a taxi arrived to take us all to our new residence. Marina and I helped load up the taxi by taking responsibility for putting our few toys in the boot. It is very reassuring to me now, that all our worldly belongings easily fitted into a taxi, including the three of us and the driver, yet we lived like we had it all and we were very happy just the three of us.

Ryde

We were all in the taxi, safely on our way to our new flat in the town of Ryde, on the corner of Buckingham Road. The thought of living in a brick house again was very welcome indeed. Within thirty minutes we arrived at the house. It looked very nice and bright, with

freshly painted white windows and new guttering. The house had a small front town garden, but none at the rear as I remember.

The first and most striking feature for me was not the house at all, but the huge conker tree opposite the house, now long gone with a young one in its place. It was very impressive and so handy for a boy who had recently enjoyed and understood the pleasures of "conkering".

We lived on the first floor with two bedrooms and a kitchen/diner. Above us on the second floor lived two old men. Luckily for me, our flat was just off the shore, and not more than a five minute walk from the sandy beach of Ryde promenade. Ryde town was an awkward town for walking around because it was built on a steep hill, so I rarely went in anyway, and why would I with the seafront and all the amenities at my fingertips? I used to spend ages in the amusement arcades nudging the penny machines and would always be getting trouble for it, especially when one afternoon when I went in and saw that my mother had got a job in one. She would sit in a booth giving people change for the gaming machines. The start of my new life here was as much fun as it was in the caravan. It was from this time in Ryde that I had my first experience of "revenge".

One summer, during the tourist season, I was offered a job. If I was interested I had to be down at the beach one Saturday morning at nine thirty. My mother had arranged this for me so I was interested! (Meaning I had no choice in the matter.) I was up early and left home around nine-fifteen. The sun was already shining and the sea looked very inviting to me. As I made my way the short distance to the beach, I passed the back of a magnificent hotel. I was always intrigued by the boxes containing many different empty wine bottles from all over the world. One bottle always stood out from the others, it was a mallet shaped bottle and sometimes it was wrapped in straw. It was called Matisse. It had a lovely picture on the front of a chateau. I had in the past picked one or two up, and took them down to the beach to study them more closely. I would have done anything to have seen it for real.

When I arrived at the beach, I was amongst other children of my age and a little older. Shortly after a talk from the farmer about what we should and should not do to a donkey (!) I was presented with one, a real donkey. There must have been around ten donkeys in the donkey rides team. How special was that, very special indeed to a seven year old!

I was given responsibility of a donkey called "Aspirin" because it always gave the farmer a headache. All I had to do was hold it still, using its reins, whilst the children were lifted aboard by their parents or the donkey rides boss. When I received my passenger, I would set off and follow a large oval shape in the sand made by the donkeys in front. I really enjoyed it and would do this for hours a day. I felt very important standing barefoot in the sand wearing only my swimming trunks, and holding a wild animal by a piece of rope, then walking with it in front of everybody on the beach including other children that I knew.

The job offered to me was for the whole season and I assumed I was going to receive some money for the work I was volunteering to do. The next day when we had finished, I was asked if I would hold my donkey all the way back to the farm. Sure, that was no problem for me, as I was enjoying my work. Once in line, we set off towards the farm. The walk was a good half an hour or so and when you have been walking all day and receiving untold numbers of bites from hungry flies, it was a bit of a challenge for me, my legs and my stamina.

The following day was much the same and so was the next. On the Tuesday we walked back to the farm using the same route as before. This time was a much more interesting trip back, as I was making friends with a girl who was a little older than me. We walked side by side, me trying to talk about seaside stuff and she was trying to talk to me about horses and those fly-bitten donkeys.

When we arrived at the farmer's gates we waited for a moment for them to be opened and went through. The farmer had been hay making that day, and the nearby fields had hundreds of square bales of hay dotted all around us as we walked up the lane. Both of our donkeys, and maybe all the others, had to be held firmly as any donkey smelling freshly cut hay will be off to scoff as much as it could if left alone. So we had our hands full until we got to the stables again.

I was now just hanging around doing nothing at all but waiting for the girl I had walked up with to finish what she was doing so I could then walk back with her. She then started messing about with the horses and said she had to do some extra jobs to do, but I could stay and talk with her and keep her company if I wanted to. Well I did and I didn't, I was shattered and really wanted to go home, but the power of girls is so darn strong you just do what they want, whatever effort is required to please them. So I lingered and listened to more horsey stuff. Then she told me that it was good experience for me to help with the donkeys and her dad was happy with me helping, and might give me something for my efforts the coming Saturday. So this girl's dad was the donkey's owner and the farmer.

I was very impressed, but wanted to talk more on the issue of money. So I asked how much the other children received for doing the donkey rides and bringing them back to the farm. She told me all the helpers did it for free and volunteered to work with the animals. They got many free rides during the day and didn't have to help with the mucking out at the farm or the cleaning on the beach.

"So it's all for free?" I asked her.

"Yes that's right, didn't you know?" No! I didn't know and what's more I'm not doing all this work for a free ride on a bloody donkey either.

I felt such a fool after all this time walking up and down the damn beach getting bitten by sand flies all day, for nothing! Don't get me wrong, I was happy to work and work hard if necessary and now I had a possible friendship with the farmer's pretty daughter, but I did it for the money! The sunshine had long gone by now and the temperature was dropping quickly and me being still in my shorts and sandals, I looked around and could see the light outside was starting to fade. So I told her I was off and said "Please tell your father I won't be doing the rides anymore..." She watched me as I stomped off through the farm yard and out towards the lane.

As I walked my mind was just getting more and more agitated. I had been used and made to look a fool. Well, I had an idea to balance things up a little. I pulled my hunting knife from its sheath that was hanging on my belt and made my way across to the far side of the hayfield. I then started to cut the strings that held the bales tightly compressed. I cut about twenty bales before guilt and fear got the better of me. The following day the farmer came to our flat and demanded to see me, but my mother would have none of it and like always, dealt with the situation herself. When I told her truthfully what I had done and why she told me off, but that was all, so maybe she understood my position.

* * *

She protected me on another occasion during the same summer, when one day I had been playing with a water pistol and after a while I was getting a little bored with it. I then had a brilliant idea that would be really funny. I decided to shoot water on holiday makers as they went by our windows, and it was as funny as hell because nobody knew where the water was coming from. This one time, a courting couple went by and I gave them the works, emptying the whole thing on them both. As before the boyfriend had no idea where the water had come from and although I was giggling while hiding below the window, it was still open so they correctly worked it out. I slowly raised my head up to the window enabling me to watch them both walk away.

To my surprise I could see him making his way to the front door. I quickly told my mother he was coming to get me and why. She told me to lock myself in the toilet and not to come out. The man came up the stairs and knocked on our door. All I could hear was the man grumbling on and demanding that I came out and apologise to him and his girlfriend. My mother told him to grow up, as it was only water and a bit of fun. Eventually the man went along his way and I was allowed out of the toilet. My mother sat back down into her chair and was laughing at the situation; she was telling me what he was saying to her at the door and then started calling him all sorts of names through her laughter.

Not much else happened whilst we lived there. One night when we were all in bed there was a terrific bang on the floor upstairs and everyone went up to investigate. Mum came down and said it was very sad but one of the old boys had just collapsed on his bedroom floor and died. I wanted to go up and have look at him but she wouldn't let me go, and I never saw anybody take him away. I must have fallen asleep.

***

Just to add one last thing, my mother took us down to the beach at around ten o'clock one very hot summers evening and told us to take all our clothes off, as did she, and we went "skinny-dipping" together. It was dark and there was no one else where we were. As we ran about screaming and shouting I was bitten on the toes by a crab and that slowed us down, as we couldn't see what we were running on or into, putting an end to us blindly running about.

The next move proved to be the last for my sister and I, though this time at least we remained in the same area; in fact, we never left Ryde. The new flat was a twenty minute walk up the hill and along the west side. But fortunately still close to the sea.

I was seven now and going on eight years of age. I was now much more adventurous than ever before. The flat we now moved into was part of a real mansion called Coniston House, half way along Spencer Road and at the top of Coniston Drive. It was a massive place; it had three floors and accommodation way up at the top in the attic. In the heyday of this house it must have had several servants, and they would have lived up there in the attic. You had to climb up two flights of stairs to get to the final door leading to the attic. You have probably worked out that this was to be our new rooms.

With my mother's inability to walk properly due to the polio she had as a child, the sight of all those stairs must have made her heart sink very low indeed. I never asked my mother how it was that she became so desperate that she had to accept this particular flat, and perhaps it's best not to. She must have been in daily agony having to go up and down during the summer months and the heat must have only added to her burdens.

In the autumn, winter and spring we would move down stairs into one of the more stately rooms. This was because the owner could rent the majority of the house to holiday makers during the tourist seasons. So we would have to move up or down accordingly. That suited us all just fine because the Christmases we shared and enjoyed where extra special because of the massive rooms and high ceilings adorned with heavy cornice work. Our Christmas tree was the biggest we ever had, but it looked quite small here.

My first experience of stealing, and suffering the consequences

We all do stupid things when we're young, but maybe we need these experiences. One school lunch time some of the boys said to me they were going to walk around the town for some fun. Nobody was allowed out of school at lunchtimes but you know how it is, if you're going out, you're going out, and this was right up my street. In fact I'm surprised looking back it wasn't my suggestion!

As we walked, two of the boys told us they were going inside the shop to get some chocolate for all to share. They went in, and sure enough we all enjoyed a share of it. The boys explained to me that they never paid for chocolate in this shop, "it's free!" they said with laughter. I asked them to explain why. "Better than that", they said, "come with us and we will show you." In we all went and the lead boy said to watch his arm and hand. He placed his right hand across the range of sweets and chocolate bars that were on display in front of him. He then picked up two identical bars one on top of the other and using his fingers he slid the top bar up his sleeve and then openly placed the other back into the display shelf. He then coolly walked out. That's brilliant, I thought!

The only experience I had of theft was when I was nearly caught scrumping apples and pears on the caravan park, and that seemed alright to me as there was plenty of fruit on the ground anyway. I had never seen anyone steal before. As bad as it was, I now began thinking if I wanted an easy taste of adventure and excitement, stealing something looked like an option. (*How some learn the hard way*)

I waited patiently until an opportunity came along permitting me to revisit the chocolate shop. The day came and I was on my own and felt fairly confident. I entered the shop and managed to repeat the training I had been given previously, and executed my mission with ease. Funny thing, guilt; though I wasn't caught in the act of stealing, I felt guilty enough never to go in the same shop again.

With my confidence in stealing growing, I found my next opportunity at home. My mother would count out her money and place different amounts in small piles on a shelf in the kitchen larder cupboard. The cupboard was a stand-alone unit with two sliding glass doors on the top and then a pull down door that became a work surface when down below was a cutlery drawer, with another two solid doors below that.

The larder cupboard was a pale blue on the outside and a faded yellow on the inside. Mother's money was always on the shelf behind the two glass doors. Eventually when my mother and Marina were out of the flat, I crept over to the cupboard and took one stack of silver coins from the middle of the row, and put the money in my pockets. I then pushed the others stacks back together and made my way down the two flights of stairs and out to the main road, which would soon take me to the shops.

It felt great having money in my pockets, and I could do so much with it, but like most boys food seemed to be the big need at first. I found myself outside one of the butcher's shops and I went in and bought myself a large pork pie. Even though this filled up my stomach, I needed more. I went into another shop and came out with a bag containing crisps, coke, and a chocolate bar with nuts in it. The only place to eat my goodies was down on the sea front next to Ryde pier. Off I walked with a smile on my face fantasising about my new found wealth! I gave no thought to the consequences of my actions while sitting on the sand with my back resting against the warm concrete sea wall. I opened my plastic bag and ate the crisps first.

There is something enchanting when you sit down in warm sunshine watching all the holiday makers playing and having fun on the beach in front of you and all around. I sat there like I owned the place! After eating my feast of goodies and with my tummy stuffed to breaking point I laid down for a while letting the sun do its thing. My eyes slowly closed and I was listening to all the sea side noises around me till I fell asleep. I didn't sleep for long for as the sun moved the sea wall cast a shadow over me and the drop in temperature woke me up.

I sat up and rose to my feet then slowly strolled off down to the beach in an attempt to let all I had eaten go down a little. I stayed on the beach for as long as I wanted, and after an hour or so thought it was time to go home. I walked lazily back up the hill. My mother and Marina hadn't returned when I got in so I just sat on the window ledge looking across the houses for something to do until they came home. Not long after, they soon appeared walking up the gravel drive to the flat carrying a few bags of shopping. I listened as they came up the stairs and walked into the kitchen; Marina dropped her bag down on the floor and sat at the table finishing off her ice lolly. I felt hard done by as they hadn't got one for me. My mother began to put the food items away in the cupboards. I had some chocolate left and I was still full, so I gave some to Marina.

My mother asked marina what she was eating and asked her where she got it from. Marina just said I had given it to her. My mother knew I didn't have any pocket money or earn any either, so she came over and asked me how I got the chocolate to give to Marina. First I told her that I had found it, she didn't believe me so I found myself explaining that the boys I was with stole it from a certain shop on the hill. She said if that was true they would not have had enough to share and still have enough left for you to bring home for your sister! Now I found myself telling her that I had stolen it and how I did it.

She was not happy and slapped me twice and grounded me for the rest of the weekend combined with other punishments. A few moments later she made her way across the kitchen towards the larder cupboard. I was in a state of worry that can only be described as "shitting myself". She went to the piles of coins and made some tutting sounds and then started moving the piles of coins around the shelf on which they were sitting. I was crouched right down on the settee with my knees up tight to my chest and chin.

It went silent for a second or two then it all kicked off. She shouted to me "Have you taken any money from here?"

"No," I said.

"Look at me" she screamed! I repeated that I hadn't touched it. "You fu----g little liar, you thieving little bastard!" She then ran over to the copper that had washing inside and pulled out the copper stick. The copper stick was used to stir cloths in the boiling water. It had become bleached white in colour, about forty millimetres thick and was just over half a metre in length. After much use in the boiling water within the copper and the detergents used, the stick had become fibrous from the middle to the very end.

My mother got hold of this stick and began raining it down on my head, my face and all over my body she was in a frenzied attack and I tried my very best to protect myself from being struck by using my arms and hands to shield myself, but she as hitting them as well. Even Marina was pleading for her to stop and no matter how she pleaded and cried my mother just kept hitting me. Eventually I started to feel light headed and lost sense of what was happing. I think I fainted or was knocked out, whichever it was I woke up in my bed in the dark and on my own. I never stole again.

Ferries

One evening my mother told us she might have found a new boyfriend and that she liked him very much. She told us she had met him at the amusement arcade down on the promenade. She said he lived in Portsmouth and had son my age. He came to the Isle of Wight for the first time since he and his wife had split up three years earlier. The suggestion was for us to go to Portsmouth on the ferry to meet him and his son to see how we all got on.

I loved going on the ferry and this was more interesting to me than mother's boyfriend. The ferry crossing was just as I had hoped for and more. I went off on my own when the ship was at sea smoothly gliding through the water. I walked every level and climbed every stairway. I was in the café one minute, and the next outside at the front then as far back to the rear as I could get. On my way to the rear again a deck hand came out of one of the metal doors and walked off, leaving the door slightly ajar. I opened the door and looked inside. It was incredibly noisy in this doorway and all I could see was the metal grid floor, which quickly came to a set of metal steps that went down further into the noise. The noise was coming from the engine room down below me. Though I was unable to see the engine room I was not far from it. I made my way down the first set of steps and was surrounded by large and small pipes leading everywhere throughout this room. I was now able to taste the diesel oil fumes that the ship fed on to sail from one port to the other.

The noise was unbearable and I wasn't sure if I had the courage to go any further. As I peered into the machine room I could see many interesting things; large metal boxes with a multitude of different coloured lights brightly shining and some flashing. As I continued looking all around me there just seemed to be an endless amount of pipes and an oily mess everywhere. Then a hand came down onto my shoulder and the deck hand that had recently left through the door was behind me, and to my relief was smiling and escorted me out to find my mother where we were reunited.

We met with this man and his son and spent the day and most of the evening in Portsmouth at the fairground. It was dark now and getting late so we said our goodbyes and made our way to the ferry terminal without him. I am unable to remember this man's face or anything about his son. But one thing I have never forgotten was his words to me when he gave me a gift as we left. The gift was a lovely looking clay pipe. It was white with long neck and a red tip. He claimed it was very old as he presented it to me very gently. He knelt down to my level and explained to me how fragile it was and that whatever happened in the future, I should remember him and the gift as it was now my responsibility to look after it. I was very touched and embarrassed then, but now I appreciate it very much indeed.

My mother was keen to get a move on, for the last ferry going across to the Island was only a few minutes from leaving the docks so we had to be sharp on our heels to get there in time. We sped off in the direction of the ferry terminal and my mother ushered us down the corridor and out onto the gantry. I can only assume she had been drinking that night for something was very wrong with our ferry. As the ferry cast off I realised it was the wrong ferry. I said to my mother this ferry is all green and only one deck and a car deck at that! She looked around in a sleepy stupor. She spoke to the ferry crew and they confirmed her error. "I'm sorry" she said "I have got us onto the Gosport ferry." Now we would have to come back on it again as we were stuck. It was midnight.

I know this because the last ferry to the Island was the midnight ferry and we watched it leave the port while we were on our return journey on the wrong ferry. When we arrived back at the harbour we had departed from an hour ago, we had nowhere to go. The next ferry would not be here until seven in the morning. My mother was a survivor and she took us to the main railway station. It was dark and getting cold. Marina and I were too exhausted to worry about our situation. We entered the station which was deserted except for a couple of drunks and a stray cat.

The lights in the station were all off except the ones at the entrance. My mother eventually found a railway man and explained our plight to him. He in turn called for another man to assist us. To my mother's credit she had persuaded them to allow us to sleep on one of the trains for the night. I clearly recall this kind man retrieving a key that was hanging on a chain attached to his belt and putting it into the carriage door unlocking it for us to enter. He then locked it again and re assured my mother that he would be there in the early morning to let us out before the train departed for Southampton. The material and fabrics chosen for the passengers to sit on was never designed for the comfort of a child's face. But sleep we eventually did.

In the morning the man at the station woke us up when he unlocked our carriage door and gave us all a cup of tea and some rich tea biscuits. I think my mother took us into the ladies toilets in the station to wash us, or it could have been in the ferry terminal. We sat inside the ferry as we sailed back home and nobody said much we were so tired.

Gail

It was a late spring afternoon when my mother advised Marina and I that our father had called on the phone earlier that day to ask if he could come and visit us all again at the weekend. I was not happy about this at all and protested bitterly against the idea. My mother calmed me down and explained to us that he was with a new girlfriend now and that he would not be staying over. And the reason he wanted to visit was to see us children and to introduce us to his new partner whose name was Gail.

I am unable to describe my feelings when I heard my father was with a new lady, it was as if he had abandoned us fully and had a life of his own, a better life without us in it. It seemed that somehow our future had been forgotten and it was no longer his concern. That's quite peculiar as I didn't want any part of him in my life any more.

The weekend quickly came along. Mother had made us wash and scrub ourselves for the big day. She had also made herself look like I had never seen her look before. She looked totally different with her hair all shiny and neat; she had make up on, and even lipstick. I didn't recognise her flowery dress either; she really had gone to town and looked stunning. Eventually a car pulled up on the gravel drive and it looked quite new, and that was impressive. We were all jostling for the best position looking out of the small attic window with eyes transfixed on the driver's door. We watched with a tension that you could almost touch.

As the driver's door opened my father got out and stretched his arms then he looked all around and eventually up at the window. He smiled and waved while shouting hello to us all. He then opened the rear passenger door and to our joyful surprise let out a golden

Labrador dog. While holding the dog on its lead he opened the boot of the car and retrieved some wrapped gifts for us.

Then the front passenger door opened and to our amazement, out got an extremely good looking blonde lady. Her hair was the same colour as the dog and she was smiling up at us too. We were all shocked and looked at each other when she lifted a small boy out from the rear seat. He was eighteen months old. His name was Gary, and it was Gail's son from her recent marriage in which her husband had died. Marina and I had forgotten our concerns and both became quite excited. My mother was more subdued in her manner and I could see she was upset to see my father with this woman. I looked at my mother and pulled my lips into my mouth to make some sort of acknowledgment of her discomfort and then walked over to her and clasped her hand. My mother responded by cuffing the top of my head gently with her right hand and pushed me playfully away.

There really was nothing I could do about the situation before us, so Marina and I rushed down the stairs to welcome them, especially the dog. My father was not the sort of man to hug or embrace his children in any manner and I knew this, so we just said hello and shook hands informally. He introduced us both to his lady friend and we shook her hand too. She said hello nice to meet you both and told us her name was Gail. It was a little awkward for us all but the dog was the distraction I feel we all needed.

I explained to Gail that my mother was unable to come down the stairs and then back up because of her bad feet and we should all go up to our flat. We all came trundled back up the two flights of stairs, dog as well. Gail was amazed we lived up in the roof and you could see an expression of anguish on her face, either that or she was knackered treading so many steps!

My mother was ready and waiting for us, she was standing arms folded with her back against the larder cupboard. She politely smiled and made everyone a cup of tea and we all sat around the dining table. Marina and I left the table to mess about with Bella the dog, leaving the adults to carry on talking about adult stuff. Eventually the conversation at the table drew to a close and Gail suggested we children should go down to the beach for the rest of the day. We agreed and where keen to do so. My mother stayed back at the flat while Gail and my father took us for a long walk along the beach. At first I wasn't allowed to take charge of the dog but after explaining about my seaside job with the donkeys Gail convinced my father to let me have Bella. We had a nice walk and I showed them where my other job was on the trampolines. The rest of the day went smoothly enough. I remember it was still light when my father and Gail decided it was time for them to go home and them getting in their car and waving good bye to us all.

***

"I thought slippers were for old people to wear on their feet, I found one school used them for hitting pupils with"

This incident was not so bad but it's funny how the unexpected often happens. I was playing marbles in the playground with a couple of bigger boys. The results would work out fairly even throughout the game and all was well. Then one of the boys left the game and took his own marbles with him. The boy left with me seemed very competitive and made it quite clear that if he could, he would win all my marbles; even my favourite ones that I would show off and not play with.

Well, he kept on and on, trying to collect my marbles for trophies and each time he won one, he would shout out aloud so all the other boys in the playground could hear and join in his victories. He had been cheating me out of my prized possessions. I hadn't noticed at first but then it dawned on me. I protested and demanded all the marbles that he had won off me to be returned to me straight away. He just laughed at me in the face. So I gathered all the remaining coloured glass balls, both his and mine, of the playground and threw them over the wall. I then pushed him over on his arse, and as he fell all the marbles in his hands fell also. Before he was back on his feet I had found all his large ones and some of the smaller ones too. Before he could stop me I threw them over the wall also. Then he and I started fighting.

A teacher intervened and took us both to the headmaster whose name was Mr Fell. After hearing both sides he told the bigger boy to go back to his classroom, and told me to stay in his office. He left me and went over to his desk. He opened one of the drawers and to my surprise he pulled out a single slipper and began walking back towards me holding it in his right hand whilst bending it over in half with his other hand. He said that he believed I had been silly in throwing another person's property over the wall and I was therefore the worst offender and he would not tolerate such mindless behaviour in his school. I was then told to bend over his table and he then used the slipper to hit me several times on the bottom. I would not cry in front of him because I didn't want him to think it hurt and my hatred of him helped me not to cry. But when I was outside his office and making my way to my classroom the odd tear did slip through.

It was now approaching the height of summer and we were soon to be on our six weeks school holidays. My mother was pleased, I'm sure!

***

One afternoon my mother was on the phone to my father whilst Marina and I played upstairs.

Mother shouted down to us, "Your Father wants a word with you." Marina and I looked at each other and walked down both flights of stairs as our mother was walking up them. When we were down we walked across the black and white tilled hallway to the phone that had been left dangling where she had just left it. Still looking at Marina, I picked up the phone and said, "Hello?" We then spoke for a while and Marina a little too. He came back to me and spoke a little more seriously, and asked "Do you and Marina want to live with me and Gail?"

I looked at Marina in shock and disbelief. I repeated his question to her as clearly as I'd received it. She was very confused also and looked a little frightened. I felt sorry for her and didn't know what to say; I needed a moment to digest the options. I passed the phone to Marina to give me a little more time, and so she could speak to him herself. While Marina was talking to him I ran up the first flight of stairs and stood on the first floor landing and shouted to my mother what my father had just asked.

She came to the banisters on the second floor and replied "it's up to you" then after a short pause said "do what you want." I ran down the stairs and back to Marina, where she handed the phone back to me. Just a minute, I said to my father, while Marina and I have a talk about it. Pressing the phone hard against my leg so he wouldn't be able to hear us we nervously debated the idea.

We said yes.

***

It was towards the end of July when my mother took Marina and I on the ferry back to the mainland, and this time we had a suitcase each!

We took the midday ferry to Portsmouth, and not much was said as we boarded the vessel. This short voyage was the reality that our time on the Island was nearly over. During the next hour our crossing of the Solent turned out to be a quiet one for me but became a little upsetting for Marina too.

We both looked back as we really were leaving a much loved and wonderful, eventful history behind us, literally. I remember spending the whole journey holding onto the railings with my chin resting on my hands looking back at the Island. I could see all the familiar land marks that I walked to or played on. I could see the buildings I would walk past nearly every day. I started to reflect on the trips my mother would take us both on; Sandown, Ventnor, Newport, Shanklin and what discoveries and fun we had. In my mind's eye I could see every detail as if it was happening in front of me. The pier at Ryde soon became a tiny structure and almost indistinguishable as I reflected our arrival a couple of years earlier and meeting Frank.

As we sailed away, the town buildings of Ryde became smaller, and I was able to recognise less and less. The Island started to lose its grip on me as it became less defined; it looked as if by magic it was becoming a soft mound of hazy colours slowly fading away. I wondered what lay ahead.

We had no idea what to expect when in the next couple of hours we would be joining my father in London. He had arranged to collect us from the station and would drive us to his new house in Hemel Hempstead or Haslemere. When our train pulled into the station I was pleased to see him waiting for us behind the ticket barriers. Marina had our cases passed down to us by the couple who escorted us to London and we walked down the platform. On our way down the platform I was feeling a little apprehensive so when the steam train on the opposite side blew a truant of steam into my legs as I walked by, I started to get upset. I told him it was the steam that has frightened me, and it did, though that was not the real reason.

My father offered to drive us around the sights of London before making our way to his house. This seemed a great idea and we hadn't been in a car for ages. He drove us over the Tower Bridge and along the side of the Tower of London. He then made his way past Piccadilly Circus and then headed towards Buckingham Palace, it was all very impressive and at first we both enjoyed it. Unfortunately by the time he had decided to show us the palace, I had been feeling sick for ages but daren't say anything until the moment of eruption! As I mustered the courage to tell him I was going to be sick he did an emergency stop while shouting "hold it a second" He dashed out the car and pulled open the door. Just at that very second I puked onto the road outside Buckingham Palace. I even managed to cover his shoes! Amazingly he was able to deal with the situation quite well and then decided to take us home.

We arrived at his house in Haslemere early in the evening and, although it was late, the evening sky was still fairly light. The house was a three bedroom detached property, and quite modern. We pulled up onto the paved drive. We were pleased to get out and stretch our legs as my father walked us up the path and in through the back door. Bella was the first to great us with her tail wagging. It was nice for us to see her too, so we made a bit of a fuss of her. The next person to come over to us was Gail, who welcomed us in and introduced us both to her mother, who was still sitting on the sofa in the living room. She never got up to greet us, she just said hello and made a polite gesture.

What caught my eye was Gail's young child on the floor in front of Gail's mother. This could have explained her not getting up, but that was a thin excuse as far as I was concerned. Gail's mother then looked across to the pair of us standing in the kitchen and said "You needn't think you're coming here to laze about, this is not a holiday camp like you've been used to, here you will work" (*Nice!*)

The young child could not sleep because of his teething. Well I knew nothing about teething or what I could do to help out as we had no experience. It was suddenly obvious that Gary the toddler was the centre of attention and that we were no longer the special ones, which was a difficult moment for me. We were shown to our rooms and laid our suitcases on the floor. We started to unpack but were told that it could wait until the following day as we had been travelling and must be tired, so we were encouraged to go to bed early that night. After we were left alone I crept out of my bed and went to the hallway to listen to what they were saying about Marina and me. It was not encouraging.

Gail had pre-arranged our school attendance and it was good fortune that the school we went to was no more than ten minutes away. My father soon demonstrated that his disciplinary ways had not diminished. During one Sunday dinner when we were all eating he asked Marina to sit up straight whilst eating. He asked her several times and then without any fuss he got up and left the table. On his return he had in his hands a broom stick, he made his way over to Marina and without any regard to her feelings placed his hand into her neck collar and violently pulled the collar away from her neck. He then again without any regard for her discomfort rammed the broom stick down her back to the seat of the chair she was sitting on. He then placed his hands upon her shoulders and pulled her back into the back of the chair. Marina was now crying and was consequently told to be quiet and to finish her dinner sitting up straight, which she tried to do. I daren't say a thing or move except for my knife and fork.

My father devised a work rota that we had to follow and abide to. This was designed to enable Marina and I to earn coloured stars for the duties we undertook. Something like one yellow star for every

100

time I washed up, then five yellow stars was the equivalent to a blue star, five blue stars were equal to one gold star and five gold stars equalled a five pound cash prize. It never worked and neither of us received any money. The school was nice and formal. I was often creating short plays of naval battles and performing them in front of the class with some other enthusiasts. Nothing else of note happened here at this house except the continued awareness that Gary was to come first in everything.

We lived there for the rest of the year and then on December the fifteenth we moved to Olney back in Buckinghamshire.

Olney

Olney was an ancient village with the river Ouse flowing around its west side and along its southern boundary. Olney was famous for its pancake race and a noted poet by the name of William Cowper. One other item of note was that the village had a wider than normal high street; legend has it that the original high street was lined on both sides with houses and shops complete with thatch roofs and one year the bakers caught fire and the whole high street was burned down. So much so, that all the ruined houses and other remaining buildings were demolished and re-built further back from the road.

We lived away from the old part, in a small bungalow north of the high street at the end of a road called Dinglederry. We had a mid-terraced bungalow with a small unfenced front garden. The rear garden was better proportioned but sloped downwards halfway along its length making it unpractical for many games. Marina and I quite liked bungalows and do to this day.

***

Not long after we moved in it was Christmas and our presents were under the tree in brown paper bags as nobody had had time to wrap them up for us. After the Christmas holidays, I had to attend my new school, Olney primary school. My new school was at the bottom of our road, so attending was a five minute walk at most. My father and Gail took me to me to school and we were asked to sit outside the headmaster's office. We had to be interviewed before I could be formally enrolled into the school.

We sat quietly whilst waiting to be introduced and I was fidgeting a little and looking all around, when I noticed the headmasters name engraved on a wooden plaque attached to his office door, to my astonishment it read "Mr. Fell!"

Surely not the same Mr Fell from my old school in Ryde on the Isle of Wight that had hit me several times with the slipper the previous year? I sat quietly for a while and was unsure whether to explain my predicament in advance of the meeting to Gail. I reckoned it would be better to attempt an explanation before the meeting than during it. Nothing else I could do for I was certain that when I went into the headmaster's office he will most certainly recognise me and say something about the incident.

As I was halfway through telling my father and Gail my tale of playing marbles, Mr. Fell opened his bloody office door and invited us in. He shook my father's hand and we all sat down. I could see it was the same headmaster straightaway, and so to start with I kept my head down slightly. My father explained I had been to school in Ryde and that maybe we knew each other! (*Parents can be such a pain in the arse at times*)

Changing schools was becoming a real drag to me by now. Always the same thing would happen. For a start nobody would talk with you let alone invite you to join in with their games. Secondly the bigger boys only saw you as a method for them to demonstrate to any onlookers how mighty and tough they could be with aggressive behaviour towards me. In most cases it was a mental style of bullying, but others had to have some physical violence sprinkled in to the cruel mixture.

I could clearly see from the expression of the many onlookers that both methods of bullying had a good effect on them. During one lunchtime, the older boys taught me some new words and encouraged me to repeat them to Ms Sutton, who was on playground duty at the time. She was a big fat lady who taught us English. I knew the words I was about to use may be rude but I had never heard them before so had no idea what I was saying. I duly approached Ms Sutton and delivered a short sentence.

Her face was a picture of both pain and hysteria at the same time. She slapped my face and told me off. I was then lifted up by my trousers and frogmarched to the headmaster's office. The older boys had their fix and I endured them laughing about it for several days. Shortly after this incident I was in the playground when I saw the bullying boys all sitting on the ground with their backs against the wall soaking up the sunshine. The smallest of the gang was sitting in the middle of his friends and called me over to him.

At first I ignored them, but they persisted and got louder in their demands. I walked over rather cautiously and stood in front of them. The small boy said "come over to me closer" and I did, "No, closer" he said again, and now I was toe to toe, "Now bend over I want to whisper something in your ear" he said quietly. How stupid was I. I lent right over and he suddenly grabbed my chest and nipples together and squeezed tightly. I was in agony but did not flinch. He quickly realised I was not going to provide him with the satisfaction of me squealing, so he increased his grip to his full strength. I was enduring excruciating pain but I still didn't make a sound or facial expression. He realised he could not inflicted any more pain onto me so held me for as long as his strength would hold out. He then twisted his fingers off my nipples and laughed as I walked away. I walked slowly along the playground and around the corner where the toilets were and ran into the first cubicle. I closed the door and roared my eyes out trying not to massage my chest as it was too painful and sore to touch.

I eventually managed to pull myself together and picked myself up off the toilet seat. I knew my red, tear-soaked face would give the game away that I had been crying a lot, so instead of returning to the classroom when the bell went, I made my way out of the playground and walked off through the streets to the abandoned railway station to explore its many rooms and hidden secrets.

Old Olney railway station was a fantastic place for us boys to play in and around. It was a picture postcard station with all the typical features and fittings you would expect for an important Victorian railway station. The station had been abandoned for a year or so and all the railway lines had been removed with the wooden sleepers, only the chippings were left.

When I went into the station I was surprised the doors were unlocked and open. You could just walk and around in complete freedom. It was if the people who had worked in it had left a few weeks ago and nobody had been in to deface or vandalize it in any

way. In fact, the safe was still in the main office and most rooms still had some remaining furniture. I do remember hundreds and hundreds of letters and envelopes strewn around the attic floor, and I would shuffle my feet as I walked through them. I did pick a few up and found envelopes dated from the forties, but never picked any up to take home or keep as souvenirs. I wish I had.

The most exciting game my friends and I enjoyed at the station was with air pistols and air rifles. I never owned one but the other boys did. At first the games were quite straightforward enough. We would place a bottle on some old abandoned car or van dumped in the marshalling yard at the rear of the station and then we would take it in turns to smash them.

One weekend I had a much better idea, though I now know better, and I think it was totally irresponsible at that time. The new game involved us splitting into two groups. Then we flipped a coin to see who remained outside and hid amongst the dumped vehicles they had to place as many glasses bottles on top of the vehicles. The other group went into the station. The group that had the station went in and slid open all the sash windows at the rear and placed all manner of glass bottles on the window ledges. On the word "go" we had to fire at each other's bottles and the group who lost all their bottles first were the losers. Skill, fear of blindness and other emotions went through us all and not a single one of us was hurt during the shootouts.

Unfortunately our fun was to be interrupted by a completely stupid act from some out of town lad new to the group. When we had finished smashing each other's bottles we decided to go to the river for something to do. As we left the station along the empty tracks three boys were coming towards us returning from the river. We did know them but they didn't hang around with us. As we got closer to them they shouted to us and asked what had we been doing up at the station. Shooting, what? Said one of the three lads again, as we shouted back our previous reply the out of town kid held up someone's air rifle and pointed it straight at the boy shouting at us.

Without any warning the boy with the rifle pulled the trigger and fired straight at the face of the other boy. We were shocked by his reckless action and horrified when the boy collapsed to the ground, yelling in pain while holding his face. We all ran over, including the boy from our group who shot him. We managed to help the poor lad up to his feet and had a look at his face. The pellet had hit him just beneath his bottom lip. The pellet was deep inside his skin and no way could anybody even try to get it out for him. The pellet had also broken one of his teeth. After about fifteen minutes or so the injured boy had calmed down and was admiring his damaged face in one of the mirrors hanging off one of the abandoned vans.

He went off home to have it sorted out. An hour later his dad arrived and gave us all a hard time. The boy who did the shooting had long gone, much to this man's annoyance. We never played those games again.

*　*　*

I had one final and painful experience before I was able to settle down within my new school. After one play time we all made are way into our respective classrooms. I was far from the first few into my class, but was never the last. Most of us were now sitting down and waiting for the stragglers to arrive, and Mrs Shaw our teacher. One of the popular boys was sitting amongst the girls showing off as usual. He got up from his chair and made his way across the classroom towards me. I was sitting in the middle of the front row of desks at a right angle to where he was sitting. When he got to me he said he was going to pick me up by my ears. I said nothing and just looked at him; he lent over with his shirt in my face and clenched my ears in a firm grip. He commenced lifting them up, I gave no resistance as I thought he was only fooling around trying to impress the girls and this was just him teasing me.

I was wrong, he then actually pulled my ears so high my head almost left my body and with a loud crack and in excruciating pain in both ears I reacted. I sprang up from my desk, pushing him off me and onto the floor; I jumped over my desk and got to him as he was getting up laughing at me. I grabbed him by one ear and dragged him back to his desk as he was begging me to let go. I then threw him at his chair where the girls were sitting screaming. Just at that moment Mrs Shaw arrived and called me to the desk to explain, and I did, exactly. We were both escorted to Mr Fell's office and sat on a short bench outside awaiting his audience. The other boy looked at me and apologised which surprised me. I wasn't bothered with his apology at that moment, but later we became friends.

Word must have got around the school, for never again was I bothered by anyone whilst I was there or when we moved up to the middle school just up the hill.

***

My first friend that I can remember the name of was Colin Welch; his uncle had a transport company, and was apparently well known in the area. I was new, so not bothered who he was or who he was related too, we just had so much in common at that time. We spent most our school time and home time doing as many exciting and adventurous things as possible. We would jump from the railway bridge into the river Ouse where nobody else would dare. We would chase bullocks into the river just to watch them panic as they ran in. We had no worries about picking up cow pats and threatening to throw them at the girls. We would swim for ages around the bridge and other scary places especially through tall green reeds and we would advise others to keep away from them in case they should get tangled up and drawn under; even though nothing was further from the truth, they all believed us! We often climbed the taller trees and passers-by would worry for our safety and try to talk us down. Sometimes we would find two trees close to each other that we could both climb and we would race up as quickly as possible to outdo one another. We had favourite trees we would often re-visit to climb and then would just sit up there chatting for ages.

During one of our summer explorations into the countryside surrounding our village we discovered a massive mound of earth maybe the size of a tennis court. It was plain to us that this was no ordinary mound for it had a door allowing access into it, so we reckoned it must be a nuclear bunker or even a military arms storage facility left over from the war. It was hidden beneath a massive grassy mound at the top of the lane that ran alongside the convent. It was surrounded by a tall black mesh security fence with three rows of barbed wire on the top. This was no obstacle to us, the intrepid heroes of adventure! We quickly found its weak spot and managed to find our way through and while both laughing we raced each other up its steep sides.

After a struggle we managed to get on top of the mound and we both looked down to where we had climbed and smiled with a sense of achievement. To our surprise the top was flat and there was even grass up here. As we walked around we saw several black pipes sticking up about four inches across and a foot high. I also noticed several black and rusty manhole covers. I said to Colin let's try to lift one, it could let us into this chamber which is bound to be full of stuff. At first we struggled but then I ran down the bank and found an iron bar that we managed to force into the gap around the manhole. With great excitement we managed to lift one of the hatches and peered in. The first thing we noticed was the sound of splashing water beneath us, then as the lid was pulled clear we both peered into the darkness and for a moment could see nothing but total blackness.

Then Colin said he could see our faces reflecting in the water below us. I pulled him back so I could lower my head through the opening. As my head slowly dropped beneath the edge of the hatch all I could see was just blackness and the sound of splashing. Slowly my eyes began to adjust to the dim light below and I could see myself as Colin had done. I asked Colin to drop something into the water so I could see the ripples to give me an idea how far down the water was. While he was trying to find some stones I looked all around inside this massive tank full of water. I couldn't see the extent of the tank and this made it by far the scariest place we had ever found. I reckoned to see better I should open another manhole to let in more daylight through. I pulled myself out of the hole and used the same iron bar to open the nearest one to me. When this second hatch was removed the light shone down into the clear water beneath. It was a massive area of water and alongside this hatch there was a set of iron steps leading down into, and through the water.

Now with the extra light we could see much more, and boy was it eerie and scary in there. The droplets of water echoing non-stop, and the ripples made in the water would move outward and disappear into the darkness. We dared each other to go down the steps into the tank amongst the echoing sounds that were all about, though most seemed to come from the darkness to the sides. The dare was to go down and touch the water with your foot. If we both did this task we should go back down and touch the water with our hand. A real challenge indeed, considering you would be holding onto the rung with one hand, whilst the other was stretched out to make a clear ripple for us each to see, proving we had accomplished our mission. A feat of extreme bravery in anybody's book I can assure you!

We shook hands and promised each other not to put the lid back on the manhole cover whilst one of us went down. As we had made a blood brother pact some weeks earlier this was a promise you had to keep no matter how funny you thought it would be to put each other in darkness for a moment. I mustered up the strength to go in first. So in I go, holding on for my dear, wretched little life.

As I lowered myself into the chasm of doom, the fear kicked in big time; the droplets of water dripping from the many steel girders around me made my senses uncomfortably multiply and the sense of shitting myself was never far away. I was shaking as I lowered myself down the iron rungs, my eyes were wide open like an owl, and I began to have imaginations that the entire ghost and zombie population of the whole world was living in this tank waiting to pounce on me and drag me down into the deep water below my feet.

I had to stop myself looking into the girders disappearing in the darkness and I had to focus on the clear water beneath me. The depth of the water was difficult to tell but I would think twenty-five metres would be close. Knowing the depth wasn't helping me, I just wanted you to know it was bloody deep in there. Eventually I managed to touch the water with the tip of my toe attached to an extremely stretched leg! My mission completed and the hatch still off! I promptly made my way back up and out into the welcomed vastness of space and lovely sunshine. Not surprisingly we never managed to raise enough courage to go down a second time and touch the water with our hand; once was definitely enough!

***

Next door to Colin's house was a row of disused thatched cottages and they had been abandoned earlier in the year. We managed to get in one of them to see what we could find. They were dark and damp with nothing but rubbish in most rooms. We did find a gas mask from the war and some old broken toys. We soon lost interest in this cottage and so forced our way into the others that had not been locked up.

We found ourselves messing around in the rear gardens, and rummaged around in the sheds. The sheds proved more interesting that the cottages, for people left most of their tools and plant pots behind amongst other stuff they had forgotten they had. We found loads of interesting tools, all quite rusty but so much stuff we just threw it all about as we searched for that something special. We never found it and so made off.

As we walked away I took hold of a long heavy iron bar propped up against one of the sheds. It was as long as I was tall and I held it up like tossing the caber at the highland games. I hurled it up into the sky best I could and it came down point first and hit the ground and that should have been that, but to our amazement when it hit the ground it kept travelling down and eventually completely disappeared. We looked at each other laughing in confusion and went over to investigate where the iron bar had disappeared to. We could see the hole and so moved away the grassy soil to reveal a rotten wooden well cover we jumped back and away from the cover and then crept back. We easily pulled the rotten timber apart to reveal the deep well below. In the narrowness and darkness we could not see the iron bar so we dropped a stone into the well to figure out how far it was to the water. We could see a long way down. We told Colin's dad about it and he came round with a sheet of corrugated steel and placed it on top.

It just goes to show how dangerous old houses and their gardens could be for a couple of lads messing around in them. I think it was a lucky escape for one of us.

***

During the summer months in Olney all the kids made much use of the river for cooling down in and generally having fun, some even swam in it. I was as much at home in the water as I was up a tree. One day was to be my last it the waters of Olney. As I was splashing and frolicking around with my friends some larger lads came in the water too and started messing around the same as us. In a short time we all joined in stone throwing at each other pushing and shoving, you know how it goes. The mucking around seemed to be getting rougher to me and I thought it best to get out whilst it was still good fun. As I made my way out towards the bank one of the larger boys called me back in. I explained I had to be home now so was off before I got into trouble for being late. He was now pushing through the water after me laughing and telling me to hold on and come back because they were going to play a game with an old tyre and I would make up the team numbers

I refused and kept making my way to the bank. He must have got the hump because the next thing I was under the water with my face banged on the large stones on the river bed. I got up and took a breath trying to shake him off me. He held me tightly and said "oh, so you want to fight do you?" I said not, and asked for him to just let me go. He pushed me under the water again and held me there for a moment. I freaked out and managed to get him off me with my tummy all cut and scratched as well. His grip on me was lost; I popped up out of the water and pushed myself away from him. I was getting my breath back he came walking through the now muddy water towards me again.

By now everybody in the water and on the bank was watching us. He got closer and closer, I didn't move this time, I just stood there waiting for him. He must have sensed my attitude had shifted and when he stood in front of me he didn't make a grab for me this time, he just started teasing me. I realised he was having a double think so at that moment I punched him as hard as my arms could deliver my clenched fist straight into his thin bony face and across his long nose.

As he held his nose in his bloody hands, I smacked him hard in the face again. He started to defend himself by trying to duck away from the blows and then he tried to grab my arms in an attempt to stop the raining blows. Eventually this he managed to do, and we both rolled in and under the water wrestling with each other. This was quite frightening for me but he just wouldn't let me go and I just wanted to hit him again and again. His friends came over and pulled us apart but as I was still going for him and he wouldn't let up. He wanted to get even with me but the older boys separated us and escorted us both out of the water and up onto the bank. We must have looked like two famous boxers going into the ring.

A massive ring of children of all ages surrounded the pair of us chanting "fight-fight-fight" it was quite barbaric and intimidating really. We moved around the arena waiting for the other to make a move. He knew I would punch him again and was hesitant to get close to me. I didn't want to wrestle with him because he was bigger than me and could easily have pinned me to the ground and punched me to a pulp.

I was not so sure if this was a good place to be. Next thing, a short boy with short blond curly hair, blond eyebrows and piercing blue eyes pushed his way through the crowd and stared at me. He made himself known to me by telling me, he was the elder brother to the boy in front of me and he was going to ensure it would be a fair fight. He then assured me his brother would win! I decided not to fight, what was the point. I had beaten him in my mind and was sure he knew it and that would do me. I was unsure what lay ahead if I continued and so I told the blond boy so, to my relief he got my hand and his younger brother's hand and made us both shake and that was it, all over. We did shake hands and I walked away without any cheering or clapping as they all watched me go, glaring at me, and they all stayed on the bank.

Over the years I have been to Olney many times and often driven along the road leading to the playing field leading to the bend in the river where we used to play. I have never been back to the spot down the river's edge. One summer's day I would like to pop along and maybe sit on the bank and reminisce, not on my own though!

***

All my class were due to move up to the middle school and so we had a pre move visit. The middle school was massive compared to ours and everybody was excited by the move. Some other children joined with us who we didn't know but we all settled down quite soon. One of the new boys was called "bogie Ollie." He was a tiny, skinny little chap, more like a ferret really. It wasn't long before I realised why Ollie was called Bogie Ollie! (*Dirty little bastard.*)

114

There was a boy who started school with us from another county, his name I can't recall but he quickly became well known to us all. It was claimed by other boys that this new lad had two willies. Something we all wondered about, He looked normal to us and I would say better looking to the girls than us lot. During some lessons this boy would need to go to the toilet and the teacher would always nominate someone to go with him and stand around making sure he was all right. One afternoon I was nominated to escort the boy, I was intrigued and embarrassed at the same time but really I wanted to see if he really did have two willies.

So off I went with him to the little boy's room that was built outside in the playground, and it was blooming cold that day. I opened the door for him and in we both went. I leant against the far wall while he made his way to the trough. Once he got there he seemed to struggle a little getting out his best friend and no way was I going over to help him get it out. So I left him to it. After several minutes he was sorted and I could hear him peeing. The cold room we were standing slowly began to fill with the pungent smell of dead fish and if was filling my nose so much so I squeezed my nostrils tightly together. I looked at the boy peeing and just knew the smell was coming from him.

I watched him as he started huffing and puffing in discomfort. The smell was awful and I could see steam coming from his pee; I just had to go over and see for me what he had wrong with him and if he really did have two willies. I held my nose even tighter and went to him and stood next to him. I looked down and saw his willy. Oh my god! To my shock and disbelief he had pee coming out in several different places and had holes all over his penis. God knows what he had wrong with him but whatever it was, god bless him. I asked "you alright mate?" but he said nothing and kept looking down at what he was doing. Shortly after he finished we made our way back to the classroom saying nothing to each other as we walked through the freezing playground. (*No, we didn't wash our hands*)

As I sat at my desk I was asked by girls and boys, did I see anything? Is it all true? I am proud to say, I said I had seen nothing, because I was too far away from him. I generally felt compassion for him and was not going to be the one to make his poor miserable life any worse than it already was.

* * *

The bungalow next door to ours had been for sale a while and must have now been sold as we watched the removal lorry back up and the men unload furniture and other contents. A few hours later, when they had gone we heard our new neighbour in the house. We wondered for a day or two who it was because we never saw anybody. Then my English teacher, Ms Sutton, turns up and put a key in the front door. Oh no, it's my English teacher living next door and she hates me.

Back at home things were much the same as always my sister and I kept ourselves to ourselves and out the way as much as possible, it was winter now and we had many frosty nights and early mornings. It wasn't long before the snow started falling and settled all around us. During this time my father obtained a kitten from somewhere, why is anybody's guess. We only had it for one day! I remember every one wanting to fuss the kitten and my father was getting fed up with us chasing it and it running all over the bungalow trying to escape our attentions. He eventually cornered the kitten. My farther explained to us how, cats had nine lives and although this little chap was small, it was a strong little survivor and to demonstrate he was going to put the kitten outside in the snow so it could do its thing. This he did and we all laughed as it tip toed across the fresh snow. It did what it had to do and came back to the patio doors. It cried and pawed at the glass to be allowed back in to the warmth.

My father told us to leave it alone as it was doing fine and a little more fresh air won't hurt it. He must have become angry with its crying, for one minute he was sitting down reading his favourite newspaper, the "Times" and the next he was up and outside holding the kitten. We then watched him as he threw it up onto the roof and said "now shut up". Marina and I asked Gail if we could go outside and have a look at the kitten to see if it was alright. She said that was fine and outside we both went, including Gail. The kitten was whining as it walking about to and fro on the cold snow.

My father told us to come in as it was getting cold with the door still open. Later that evening we went to our beds with the kitten still on the roof of the bungalow. In the morning whilst having breakfast I asked Gail if she had seen the kitten. She said she hadn't but not to worry as cats and kittens always came home when they pleased and our kitten was no different. After I was dressed and the kitten was nowhere to be seen, I asked Gail if she'd looked up on the roof for it, but she hadn't. So I went outside and looked up and scanned the snow covered roof.

Straight away I saw the kitten laying on its side with its head almost in the gutter. "Can you see it?" shouted Gail?

"Yes" I responded, "its dead and frozen stiff as a bone". I stood for a while looking at its face and asking, how could they go to bed leaving this kitten up on a snow covered roof all night? When Gail told my father the kitten was dead, he came out to see for himself and made some feeble excuse.

He reached over to the washing line prop and nudged the kitten off the roof and told me to bury it. This task proved to be impossible as the ground was frozen. Without saying a word I dropped it into the garden waste burner where it stayed until the thaw. When the frosty weather changed to mild, we soon remembered where the dead kitten had been placed!

***

I hadn't played truant from this new school, because I had made friends and was settled in quite comfortably. My friend Colin lived just at the bottom of our road next to our school and his dad was the park keeper at a local sailing club based in Emberton Park, just outside the village. One morning while I was in Colin's house before we went off to school, Colin told me he wanted to help his dad collect the rubbish from the lakes and he wanted to go that morning because it was a warm and sunny day. He asked me to join him and I was keen to do so. We decided to change our clothes and I borrowed some of Colin's. We waited until the school playground was empty and the teachers had gone in. Now we could walk from Colin's house to the park, which was about two miles away.

We found Colin's dad and told him we had been allowed home that day because the water had been turned off at the school. Colin's dad gave us both a special contraption he used for picking up litter without having to bend down and pick it up by hand. Our job was to walk around the lakes and collect as much litter as we could and deposit it all into some large black plastic bags Colin's dad would collect another day. This was an easy job and we found all sorts of interesting things to keep us out of mischief. We couldn't reach some litter floating on the lakes so we went back to Colin's dad and Colin asked if we could take one of the canoes belonging to the sailing club out onto the lakes to collect the rest of the rubbish. We spent the rest of the day canoeing all around the lakes going into places nobody else would go. We forgot all about our job and began swimming about like two fish. This had to come to an end sooner or later, and when we became tired of it we made our way back to the boat shed. With the canoe returned we said our goodbyes to Colin's dad and set off to our homes.

In order for me to get away with our day's truancy I needed to be home at the usual time and make out I had been to school. We arrived back in the village later than intended and I still had to get changed back into my school clothes making me even later. I was wondering if possibly the game was up for me.

Sure enough, I had blown it. Our new neighbour, Ms Sutton, had asked my father if I was poorly as I hadn't attended her English lesson and wasn't at school. When I eventually arrived home I went in and my father said nothing of this to me when I walked passed him. I put my things away as normal and had a few biscuits from the tin in the kitchen. My father asked me if I had any homework to do. I replied I had nothing that day and would like to go out to see my friends before dinner. He told me to go to my room and wait for him. His voice and manner were well known to me and I knew I had been caught playing truant.

He had developed a new form of punishment for me. Today I feel it was unnecessary and very cruel. He came into my room and quizzed me about the lessons I had that day. Like all boys I lied and lied away thinking I had persuaded him I had been to school. This was a mistake he knew I would make. So now I had well and truly made things much worse for myself. He was very angry by now and looked pleased when he informed me about the conversation he had with Ms Sutton a little earlier. He reached out and grabbed me by the shoulders and shook me violently whilst at the same time shouting at me. Gail and Marina came into the room and tried to calm things down. He let me go and told me to lie on my bed face down with just my pants on and wait for him to return. He told me that I was going to receive his belt across my arse and get hit twice for playing truant and twice for lying. I was told not to move until he said so. He would walk passed my bedroom and look in to make sure I was still on my bed. He also would make a banging noise with the belt by folding it in half and then pushing the ends together. This would make a loop in the middle of the folded belt. He would then very quickly pull the two ends away from each other and the belt would close making a loud bang.

I was left terrified for an hour at least before he came into my room. He explained his reasons for the punishment to me again and told me I had to lay still. I did as I was told and was already crying uncontrollably before the first strike. The pain I endured is beyond my ability to describe, but if you have ever burned yourself with the edge of an iron or a hot tray from the oven, that would be half the pain and discomfort. Then the second came down on me just as hard as the first and with no mercy. Poor little Marina had heard all this and was crying in the other room. I can clearly remember her coming into my room and trying to pull my father's arm down, pleading with him to stop hitting me. He told Gail to get Marina out of the way. Gail came in and she also said that was enough now, but he insisted in completing his punishment and so Gail had to take Marina out of my room and she closed the door behind her.

I still don't understand how I stayed on the bed wriggling and writhing in pain waiting for the last two strikes. In later years my sister would mention this event more than any other and it must have made an impression on her mind as well as mine. My father never apologised to me for this or any other times.

***

Marina and I used to go out on my bike, and she would sit on the cross bar. Our favourite ride was around the building site at the back of where we lived. One time we rode around and found large mound of gravel had been delivered to the site. We got off my bike and ran up the gravel. It was good fun for a while and we enjoyed messing about with all the small stones. We then decided to walk along the tops of all the house foundation brickwork. We had to place one foot in front of the other, keeping our balance. We became good at the task we had set ourselves and soon went off to find another game. After an hour or so I went back to collect my bike only to find it had been thrown into a trench full of water.

I climbed into the trench and pulled my bike out of the deep muddy water and pushed it up onto the road. When I climbed out and stood my bike up I could tell somebody had been trampling on it; both wheels were severely buckled.

I looked around the site to see who could have done this but there was nobody about except two men in a trench a couple of plots away. As I continued to look around me I heard the engine of a tractor or digger coming around the corner. I saw it was a yellow dump truck with a bucket full of gravel. The man driving was a big fat chap with a black beard. He drove the dumper truck past me and drove to the pile of gravel Marina and I had been playing on an hour earlier. He rammed the dumper up and tipped the bin full of gravel onto the same heap. As he pulled back and tipped the empty bin back down, he looked at me holding my busted bike and laughed at me. I pushed my buckled bike over to him and asked him if he had wrecked my bike. He said he had to teach me a lesson and not to play on his neat piles of gravel. I told him he would have to pay for it to be repaired and he responded using some of the words I remembered from my playground incident with Ms Sutton. I left him there as he smiled at me. When I walked past the other two men in the trench they told me the dumper driver was a mad-man and I was to be careful what I said to him.

I made my way home and found that Marina had already informed my father of what had happened to the bike. My father asked me to show him the man that did this, but I was not sure whether to tell him or not. He asked me again, who broke your bike? I explained that the driver of the dump truck had but two other men said the driver was a bit mad and dangerous.

My father walked alongside me as I took him to the man in the dump truck. As we passed the men in the trench my father spoke with them and they confirmed my story. They both pulled themselves out the trench they were working in and told my father they should come with him so they joined us. Spaghetti Western style we walked through the building site to the dumper driver. During the conversation the man denied he had anything to do with damaging my bike and he claimed he never swore at me either. My father gave me permission to repeat the language the driver used. I enjoyed being allowed to swear amongst adults, as it seemed that's what they did all the time anyway. Somehow, and I don't know how he did it, the dumper driver collected my bike from our house and within a week it was back as good as new. Result!

My first paid job was in Olney market square helping to sell war memorabilia and foreign paper money. Soon after starting my paying job....we were on the bloody move again!

The Move to Gretton

My father had been promoted at work and was now the national sales manager for a company called "Alcan". The new job was based in Wellingborough and at first he travelled there and back every day. He must have been very successful in his work for we had the news that he had bought a new four bedroom detached house with a massive rear garden in a village called Gretton, near Rockingham.

We helped to pack all our belongings into boxes and a lorry arrived to collect it all and take it to our new home. The day of the move was really sad for Marina and I, for we had made some good friends here and knew we would have to go through all this yet again! We all got into the car and made our way to Gretton. It took us around forty-five minutes to get there. The house was the biggest in the street and Marina and I couldn't believe we were actually going to live in it. It was only seven years old and the builder who built it built several other houses in the village, but this had been his own house. I had a large bedroom at the front, as did Gail and my father, whilst Marina and Gary had the two rear bedrooms.

We settled into this magnificent property very quickly and felt like pop stars. Regrettably my school was the worst school anybody could put their children into. It was called Corby Boys School, and boy was I in for one massive shock. I was now ten and joined the school in the first year. All the boys here looked totally different to the others I had joined in the past. All these boys talked about were fights and fighting every hour of the day. Who's going to get a kicking or who's just got a kicking? I wasn't sure how to begin to even try to fit in here. These boys were mean and they knew it, so it wasn't long before I became the centre of unwanted attention. I'm going to spare you endless tales of me being tormented and bullied as it may have become tiring by now. What I think is important is to tell the tale of how I stopped the bullying. No I didn't tell a teacher!

One certain chap always hit me across the top of my head when our paths crossed and it was always when he was in front of some girls. He was slightly taller than me with long blond hair and bright blue eyes and a slim build. I was always laughing at his bulling and played it down as if he was funny and it was all part of our silly fun. His slapping began to get harder and more menacing, and often made my head ache for a while. He received his comeuppance one morning though.

The classes were mixed classes now, as the boy's school had merged with the girl's school next door and egos were running high. The boy in question was not in my form, so I would only bump into him from time to time. I wasn't scared of him but I just wanted a peaceful life and chose not to retaliate unless I had no other choice. My class were all standing in the corridor waiting to go into the classroom. For some reason we had been outside the classroom for some time and people had started to mess around, myself included. I hadn't seen this particular lad walk down the corridor. The first I knew he was next to me was when he smacked me hard on the back of my head. I was a little dazed and embarrassed, for in front of me were a dozen girls or more and they were laughing with him. This recognition must have encouraged him to ramp up his courage in making a fool of me because he hit me several more times around my head.

I was just at boiling point, though he was unaware of this until he tried to hold one of my arms up to make me punch my own head. That was the spark that ignited my swift and equalising action. I pushed him back a foot or so then without stopping I grabbed his jumper at the front of his chest with my left hand and with my right hand I grabbed him by his balls and lifted him up above my shoulders and threw him into a large iron radiator hanging on the wall in the corridor. The girls started screaming and panicking amongst themselves while I walked over to him and looked down at him all crumpled up on the floor as he had bounced off the radiator. I said nothing because it was very likely we would now fight it out. I was wrong, he stood up and tidied his hair and apologised to me. I told him to apologise again so everyone in the corridor would hear him and he obliged.

When everyone was making their way into the classroom he hung around and asked me to join him to the side. I stepped out of the way for those still entering the classroom and he said to me how sorry he was and he would never mess me about again. Darn right you won't, I was thinking, as he placed his hand on my shoulder before walking away.

During the days when the school was an all boy's school, all the teachers carried with them their canes. It was a daily event to be struck like cattle in the classroom or the corridors. When the girl's school amalgamated with ours the canes all disappeared, except the ones Mr Wright had in his office. Mr Wright, or "Chocker" as he was respectfully known to us boys, was the Head Master of the boy's school and became the Deputy Head when the schools joined together.

I was eager to follow some of the playground antics, and one brilliant trick was being able to protect yourself from head butts. We used to insert as many needles and pins as we could, underneath our blazer lapels. Some pins would face upwards and others downwards. When one of the older boys was going to head butt you, he would most likely try to grab you by the lapels and whilst he had you in his grasp, he would pull you towards him as he head butted you. With the pins and needles under your lapels you could jump up when he grabbed you making the needles and pins puncture his fingers and cause him some considerable pain and discomfort so much he would have to let you go. This was a fabulous deterrent and it worked really well. Unfortunately one afternoon our religious teacher Mrs Simons had had enough of me fooling around and called me to the front of the class for a showdown. I duly obliged and received a lecture. I was made to laugh by my friend who was making suggestive hand signals to me while Mrs Simons had her back to him.

Mrs Simons became agitated at my sniggering and grabbed me by my blazer lapels. I naturally moved away from her and as I did so I saw her facial expression instantly change. She had hooked herself on the pins and needles and for a split second she was unable to let go. I could clearly see her distorted face twisting from the pain in her fingers tips. She managed to free herself and demanded I show her what I had beneath my lapels. After a few minutes' she told me to wait outside in the corridor whilst she went to sort out her fingers. She seemed to be gone for ages and when she did eventually return she had Mr Wright the Deputy Head alongside her.

He had a stern chat with me and had a close look at my blazer. He asked me to take it off and follow him to his office. I wasn't sure why I needed to go there but had no choice in the matter. When we arrived he asked me to wait outside for a few minutes as he was busy. As I patiently waited, several older boys passed by and advised me I was definitely going to get caned. This was a little worrying and the anticipation was starting to make me nervous. Eventually Chocker invited me into his nice, wood panelled office.

At first he advised me on the dangers of my defence strategy and how unwarranted the results had been to Mrs Simons. He then made his way to the rear of his desk and told me I was about to be caned. Above his desk and halfway up the wall hung a two door cabinet, very similar to the ones used in pubs to keep the dart board in. He made his way to the cabinet and pulled open the two doors. Inside was a selection of canes, all neatly place on evenly spaced pegs.

He paused, turned around and said "Can you see my collection of canes, Master Howard?"

I respectfully replied, "Yes, Sir." I looked at them, maybe five in total, some were very thin and others thicker. One was particularly thick.

"Good" he said, and then he asked me a question I shall never forget for the rest of my life. "Which one would you like to choose for your caning?" God! I thought, I really am going to get caned and in a just few moments. Before I was able to make any comment he reached up and took hold of the thickest one in the rack.

"Oh! I think this one will be the best one for you, and do you know what this one is called, Master Howard?" I had no idea and was not in the mood to play his games as I was by now bracing myself for some serious pain to land upon my arse. He looked straight at me and smiling in advance of his next line he said, "It's called the Doctor! And do you know why? Because it cures everything!" I actually thought that was very funny and laughed a little with him.

"Right," he said, "bend over the desk and pull your trousers taut over your bottom so there's no creases in them." He then made sure I had no magazines or newspaper hidden in my trousers and said "right!" I heard the cane come down swiftly cutting its way through the still air of his office. It made a similar sound to "Swoosh" then it made contact with my bum cheeks. Well, I bit my teeth together and squeezed my bum cheeks together at the same time as the sharp stinging pain travelled through my body.

I stood up and using both my hands frantically rubbed and massaged my bum. The pain and rawness was excruciating and it wouldn't abate, no matter how much my hands smoothed my bum. I was unable to look at him or do anything else as my senses were all working overtime when to my horror, Chocker's voice broke the silence as he said, "What are you doing standing up, Master Howard? I haven't finished yet."

Oh my God! I don't believe it he's going to cane me again! "Bend over, Master Howard" he said again, though this time he spoke in a demanding voice. "Swoosh" and down came the second strike and it fell in exactly in the same place as the first. Only another person who has been caned knows how the receiver feels and I can tell you it is most definitely something to be avoided! I was asked to leave the office without any more punishment. As I walked out and away I was at the brink of tears, but no way was I going to allow him to see me break down in or outside his office.

By the time I reached the boys toilets the need to cry had passed, but the inability to walk properly was clearly evident to any passers-by and to avoid people thinking I'd pooped myself I told curious onlookers that I had just been caned. I had difficulty in sitting at my desk but managed to get thought the rest of the day without much bother. I told Gail all about it and she agreed it was best not to tell my father. Later that evening I took the mirror from the bathroom wall and used it to look at my bum. Wow, that was quite impressive, as I had two long purple and blue fat bruises in lines across my arse about a foot in length. A real battle scar that I could show off to my friends.

***

I have an experience to describe my father's lack of love and caring for Marina and I, as he had no time for us at all really. Not long after we moved into the house in Gretton, my father bought a brand new car. It was the first new car he had ever bought and we had ever been inside. It was a green Volvo 144 estate. I was very impressed and would sit in it for ages playing with the switches and buttons and, of course, the radio.

I asked my friends in the village to come over and have a look too. At around the same time he also brought himself a new navy blue cashmere coat and looked very smart in it. All that may sound nice and dandy, and for him it must have been. The thing that gets me though, is while he was swanking around in his nice new car and wearing his smart coat, I was going to this tough school every morning at twelve years of age with holes through the soles of my shoes. Every morning I used to cut the cardboard off a cornflakes packet into certain shapes to place inside my shoes. I had worn through the soles and through all my socks. So much so, I eventually had hard skin on the soles of my feet, however I could still feel the pieces of grit as I stepped on them in the playground. This was not a rare incident.

Another time my school trousers became so worn in the bum, I had to find the cheapest trousers for sale in the town centre which I managed to do during one school dinner break. Gail went into town and bought them for me a day or two later. I was very pleased to have them; something new and needed was a real treat. However it turned out they were totally rubbish for me as they had not a single pocket, not one, but I still had to wear them for ages and not to mind they were bright blue!

I have many more stories of my dreadful time at this school but I am aware they could become boring so here is a list of events for another time.

Teacher hits boy in face with broken chair leg
Teacher was dunk and wets himself at his desk
Teacher fondles boy's crotch while boy sits on his desk
Making explosive's at school and a boy losing part of his hand
Boys stealing mopeds and doing them up at school
Smoking was a way of life and we were always buying single cigarettes
Dinner tokens for me and Marina

Girls fighting in school and outside
Teachers in fights
A Boy hung on spiked fence
Dinner games in the old village
Electric shocks for me
Boy steals teacher's car
My head almost in dog muck
Knives and bayonets all around the school
Truancy a new way to enjoy yourself outside school
Police and me after several truants
Girls and me on truant

***

My home life experiences at this time were no different to my other homes and schools before, though by now I was eleven coming on twelve. Some of the village lads took offence because we lived in a large house and would taunt me as I waited for the school bus outside the co-op store in our village. The most popular name for me at first was "Snobs boy", and then they adopted "Rubber lips" and eventually I earned the nick name of "TAZ" from the Tasmanian devil! A nickname I cherished, as for the first time it made me an accepted member within the group of my fellow villagers and acquaintances. I must admit, I did write my name and was excited when I would hear people ask who the heck Taz is.

Early one morning, while waiting for the school bus, one of the village nutter's called Titch came along to the bus stop with some rockets he had stolen from his dad's fireworks collection for bonfire night. I watched him as he walked a little way up the road. He placed his hand into his school bag and pulled out some of the rockets. He held one at a time in his right hand by the wooden shaft coming out the tail end of the rocket. He then lit them one at a time with his cigarette lighter. As the fuse in the rocket started to burn and sparkle he pointed in my direction, within a few seconds I watched an angry sparkling rocket making its way straight towards my face!

I laughed aloud and openly to diminish my embarrassment of him firing them at me, though luckily none hit me, the other kids waiting were less fortunate and panic set in as the rockets exploded in and around them. His funniest trick was to sneak another firework called a "Jumping Jack" into people's school bags after he lit them, the recipient would freak out as the banging and cracking would suddenly scream from his bag. Then he would panic to get the bag off his shoulder and dump it on the pavement with enormous amounts of smoke billowing out from within it. The poor kid couldn't open his bag because of all the commotion going on inside it. Eventually when the Jumping Jack had jumped its last, and then the bag was slowly opened by its owner, the contents would be examined by us all. The word Barbecue comes to mind!

I was starting to get fed up with some older boys treating me as entertainment and sooner or later something was going to kick off from me. The boy who received my attention was Martin Russell, a very well-liked boy in the village gang; he was a year or two older than me and was always mocking me and threatening me with violence of one sort or another. One winter's night I was at home watching the telly when I heard chanting coming from outside the front of the house. The chanting went on for a while and my father asked why the local kids were chanting outside. I explained it was nothing and they will soon shove off and find something else to do. Unfortunately, they just all stood there and carried on for ages. In the end I was feeling so incensed and intimidated my anger overtook any fear I may have had. I stood up and went into the utility room and put on my hard leather walking boots that Gail's mother had obtained from the second hand army store for me. I put on my donkey jacket from the same source and went outside to deal with the situation that had been developing around me and my family for several weeks now.

As I walked around the corner of our home, a shout went up "he's coming out!" I saw approximately thirty boys aged from ten to sixteen. Their gaze fell upon me in an atmosphere of high tension and anticipation of gang vengeance upon me for living in a large house. I made my way up the front garden path and to the front driveway double gates where Martin Russell was proudly standing in front of his older brother. I looked at them all as I walked and feared not one of them or the numbers, I was so steamed up nothing seemed to bother me out there that night. Their gang had formed a semi-circle around Martin and his brother as though they were about to watch a performance at the theatre.

I soon reached the gate and opened it, standing in front of me now was Martin I looked him straight in the eye and straight away I could sense he was faking his position of strength. I stood upright and ready to pounce at any second, but nothing happened. The boys started to chant "Fight! Fight! Fight!" and so on. I was fully alert and primed for making a defensive move and then attack him head on, so I stared at him and waited for something to kick off!

A few moments passed when to my surprise, Martin's elder brother told me I had to follow them to a friend's house at the top of our street because there was a streetlight outside his house and he wanted to watch us fight it out there. This suggestion broke the tension and I quickly found myself being marched off following the two eldest boys, then Martin and then me, closely followed by the cheering mob. The walk was uneventful, maybe a few stones found their way into my back but nothing more. We soon arrived at the house and street lamp as nominated by Martin's brother. Right then, this is it, I thought, and braced myself to win or lose.

I faced my assailant once more and stared at him with utter contempt. Without any physical contact or conversation between Martin and me, Martin turned to his brother and said "I don't want to fight." I was very pleased with his request though I dared not show it. I stood still and waited for the older boys to make a move and accept the decision from Martin. They did, and then they had to appease the crowd. I was offered a safe passage through the mob of idiots. I knew not one of them dared to do what I had done. I walked past Martin and made my way through.

Slowly I walked away and into the darkness of the night, it wasn't long before I was on my own again and away from everybody. I could see my father in front of me, standing in a gateway as I approached. "Oh, shit," I assumed I was in deep trouble for bringing all this bother to his house. But on the contrary, he began to explain to me, as he was sitting at home after I had left with the mob he began thinking it was incredibly brave for me to have gone alone in amongst that lot and stand up for myself. He became concerned for my welfare as he noticed the other older boy was carrying a thick stick or bar down by his side and if the fight got out of hand my father was going to step in.

He then placed his hand on my left shoulder and kept it there as we walked home. Once inside he asked me to explain to him how all this had developed and why. I was a little reluctant at first because it all seemed so daft and I didn't want to offend him. I explained I was picked on because I lived in the biggest house on the street and for some reason this was not going down well with the village boys.

The following afternoon I was walking by the village war memorial minding my own business when I saw a pushbike coming towards me, low and behold it was ridden by Martin on his way to the paper shop for whatever. I thought back to the previous evening's events that he had orchestrated against me and then backed out at the last minute. Ok, I thought, this is just me and you mate! I stepped out into the road and made my way straight towards him as he cycled towards me.

He looked very uncomfortable as he was getting closer and just as he reached me, I put out my hand and grabbed his bike by the handle bars, which stopped him in his tracks. He put his left foot down and asked me what was up, I explained we had some unfinished business to finalise and he should get off the bike. No way would he let go of the handlebars, he just looked at me and repeatedly explained that it was all a mistake and things just got out of hand. I replied that it could have been very nasty for me as there were so many boys who would have all wanted a kick or two at me and one of the older boys had a weapon with him and I was not happy about him putting me in this unfair and unwarranted position.

I let go of his bike and stepped back one pace. He knew what was coming, alright. I clenched my fist so hard my knuckles cracked and then quickly raised my arm and smacked him right in the face, making his nose explode in a cloud of blood. He staggered a little and at that moment fist still clenched as tightly as before I delivered another fierce smack in his face. He fell off his bike and tears came down his face.

At that moment and as if from a comedy show an old man on an even older black pushbike came speeding over to stop me hitting Martin any more. As the old boy got himself into a bit of a panic himself his false teeth feel out of his mouth and onto the road. He tried to catch them before they were out of reach but failed to get a grip of them. This was very funny to me and gave Martin the break in events he needed.

The old timer laid down his bike and collected his dentures and after blowing the grit off them placed them back into his mouth. He came over to Martin and picked him up off the road and made quite a fuss of him. He then focused on me for a moment or two, explaining how we should put our differences' behind us and shake hands. As odd as it must have seemed to any onlooker at that moment, we did both shake hands, and without any hesitation. I did think to myself later that day that maybe now the village gang had good reason to persecute me and seek some revenge upon me one night, but I couldn't change anything. What I had done to Martin was necessary in my book and now I had to accept the next few days would be touch and go for me.

It's strange how things turn out in our lives sometimes. Fortunately, no revenge was taken out on me; in fact everybody left me well alone for a while, and would be on their guard when I walked past any individual gang member.

***

Martin and I soon became best of friends, after that incident. His elder brother Eric, who was with Martin during the attempted gang fight, was responsible for getting me my first paid employment with the local builder where he and Martin later worked in the next village to Gretton. The lovely village of Lyddington was maybe three miles from our village, and Eric was employed as an apprentice carpenter with a well-known builder in Lyddington called H. Clarke and Son, and Martin was an apprentice bricklayer.

Eric managed to get me a job as a site labourer at first, and then a plasterer's mate and then a roofer, and I finally had a chance to become an apprentice chippy. Our friendship grew stronger and developed into a united force, resulting some years later in Martin being my best man when I married a village girl. (*How mad is all that!*)

Anyway, best to keep on track!

At the back of our house in Gretton we had a massive rear garden, thirty metres wide and almost a hundred metres long, with a concrete path running up the middle to an enormous timber pigeon loft and two brick built pigsties. My father wanted them both pulling down and the pigeon loft burned whilst all the rubble from the sties had to be wheelbarrowed to the front gates ready for collection. As was always the case, this job was allocated to me. The understanding from my father was that I had to work for at least one whole hour in the garden every day after school, and should I miss an hour or half an hour it would be added to the next day and so on. However, every weekend my work detail would have to be settled before the following Monday.

When he came home he would examine my work for effectiveness and allotted time spent on each task. If my work was unsatisfactory I would have to do it all over again there and then regardless of any plans I may have with my friends. And it was the same if he considered the time I had taken to do the task was too long.

My main job was to dig and turn over the soil so I could plant his f***ing potatoes and carrots. I hated that bloody garden, for I dug every inch and had to sieve the soil to remove all the bloody stones. Another eccentric task of his I had to follow was ensuring every single fragment of white root had to be collected and piled up onto the path so he could see I had removed them from the soil. I always remember him walking up the garden when I was doing his gardening, and standing over me.

In the beginning my friend would come around and call for me, when I explained I couldn't come until I had done an hours work he offered to help me so we could both get away. When my father realised I was getting away in half an hour due to my friend helping me he made me stay for the hour regardless of how many friends stayed to help. They soon got fed up and stopped coming round.

After the first season I received the welcome news that he intended to grass seed the first three quarters of the rear garden. He actually meant him and me. He came home one evening with a brand new red and white rotavator with four rotating discs at the front. He also had two large garden rakes and god knows how many bags of grass seeds. He demonstrated to me how to start the rotavator and how to use it effectively and not to allow it to dig too deeply into the soil, blah, blah, blah! I watched him for a while and then he let me have a go. I was surprised at how powerful this machine was and wasn't sure if I could safely control it.

When he was using it, he looked like a kid with a great toy, it looked so easy. The next week we both rotavatored the large garden, already free of stones and weeds! Then we had to rake the soil as flat as possible, a task I was doing well into the evening. Seeding was a doddle and the easiest job I ever had in that garden. I have to agree that as the grass started to emerge and slowly turn the brown soil into a haze of virgin light green I was pleased to have contributed to the new effect. Eventually the grass thickened and we had a lovely massive lawn. Guess who had to cut it! My father continued in his strict and very domineering ways right up until he became ill and eventually passed away.

To this day I have no liking of gardening in any way shape or form. I do appreciate what gardeners can do and have archived, but it's a skill I'm pleased not to be concerned with.

Farming

The back of our garden faced the open countryside with not a single house for many miles. All you could see was field after field. All this open space belonged to, and was farmed by, Mr Charles Northern, a highly respected man in his seventies then who was by then a fabulous character.

One day I was standing on the heap of rubble I had made when knocking down the pigsty watching a blue and grey tractor ploughing the field right behind our house. This particular tractor must have been old or struggling to plough properly, because the exhaust pipe sticking up and through the bonnet was billowing out stacks of grey and black smoke high up into the sky, it was more like a steam train than a tractor. Like all boys, I so loved tractors and still do! Tractors seem to have an ability to entice an audience yet really they can be quite scary.

After a while the old tractor came along the hedge row and eventually it was ploughing past our house. I could just make out the shape of the driver through all the dirt and scratches on the cab windows. When he saw me waiting he smiled and waved kindly as he passed me slowly by in a cloud of sooty black smoke. I laughed at his tractor and he laughed too in acknowledgment of his machine struggling so much. I watched intensely as he disappeared around a long shallow bend and eagerly waited to see the tractor reappear.

The next time he came around, I found myself already waving to him before he got anywhere near to me, now that's a boy who likes tractors! The driver nodded towards me and smiled again, to my joy he pulled up alongside our hedge and stopped. As he settled down he pulled a cigarette out of a tartan biscuit tin that had been resting on an old and oily rag behind his seat. He offered me one for a joke, and his laughing made me laugh too. He slid back the side window in his cab and began to talking to me. His tractor was still running, so at first I was unable to hear clearly what he was saying to me. When he noticed I wasn't responding to him he realised I couldn't hear him and I was not retarded or a simple window licker at all!

He switched off the engine apologised and told me his name was Dodd and he had been working for the same farmer since he left school fifty-five years earlier. He told me all about what he was doing and why, and suggested as I was so interested did I want to climb through the hedge and have a ride in the tractor with him and see what it was like. Yes, please! I couldn't believe my good fortune. We became good friends and I enjoyed many rides in corn trailers, mostly empty but a few full of corn. I also used to ride on the back of the seed drill; my job was to tell him when any large stones jammed up the harrows. When this happened, he would stop the tractor and lift up the harrows while I would pull out the stones and rocks.

I truly enjoyed working with the farm animals, which without question was the most rewarding to me. Mr Northern had around a thousand or so Mule sheep dispersed throughout the farm and nearly every weekend I could be involved in some task involving them. I had the lowest job of all to start with in being a human sheep dog! In the hot summers I was often sent running across grassy fields dodging tall scotch thistles, often as tall as me, and wading through thick clumps of savage stinging nettles coming up to my waist.

I would always have to run in one direction whilst the "real" sheepdog ran in the other, forming a semi-circular pincer movement. We would both be shouted at in equal measure, and at the same time treated as though we were always wrong in our responses and slow in our actions. Nevertheless, the dog and I always managed to force the sheep into the stock pens in the end. Between us we would encircle a hundred coughing and panting sheep and with total exhaustion I managed to close the gate behind them before collapsing to my knees from the heat and lying down on the cooling green grass, often covered in sheep poo.

As I burned in the heat of that summer's day, barely able to catch my breath, I felt I was going to die of heat stroke and exhaustion. As I panted for more air, I noticed one of the galvanised water troughs the cows would use, was full of water. Without a moment's hesitation I pulled myself up from the ground and made my way across the farm track and climbed over the fence. The water in the trough looked clean enough, so without taking any of my clothes or shoes off I plonked myself deep down into the cooling water. Ah! The relief was beyond description, I just laid there in total bliss for five minutes or so. As I was cooling down I leaned my arms out the side of the trough and tried to regain my composure.

I glanced across at the sheep dog looking for a united expression of achievement, but he wasn't wasting any time looking at me, his eyes were alert and transfixed to the actions of each individual sheep standing in front of him. I watched him and observed his head was precise in its every movement as he remained intensely focused in his work. I watched him closely, his pink tongue quivering as it dangled from his mouth looking like a dripping wet sock glistening in the shadows of the sheep. This collie was all black with three white feet; it was outstanding in his skill and ability. This was a top class sheep dog and I can see him now, standing at the farmer's side motionless, whilst waiting to execute his next instruction with total obedience.

It was not long before a loud bellowing voice brought me back to my senses and told me to get out of the trough and help with "dagging" the sheep; I reluctantly began to stand up. It was at this point I discovered although the water in the trough was clean, the bottom of the tank was forty millimetres deep in a stinking thick slimy black sludge!

It stank like a million rotten eggs from all over the farm had been dumped into the bottom of this one trough and squashed flat as they rotted down, Argh the stink! And it was sticking to me like thick black crude oil all over my shoes and trousers. As I began to use the water I'd been sitting in to clean myself down I became even smellier. What a state to get into, I was in a right mess, and I would have been better off staying hot and getting on with the job. I came back to the sheep pen, passing a stack of straw bales, and grabbed several handfuls of straw to wipe of the gooey mess. The farmer, Mr Northern and Dodd both found my predicament very amusing until I was working alongside them both a little later!

This day we had to "dag" the sheep. Basically we cut the wool at the back of each sheep that was covered in sheep pooh. Sheep are generally white and often their bottoms and tails go a dark green as a result of them 'getting the runs', so to speak. They usually get the runs from worms and parasites within their digestive systems. If we left the fouled dark green wool attached to them it would quickly attract many species of flies and they would lay hundreds of eggs onto the sheep's wool and into the sticky poo. Eventually the eggs would turn into maggots and they would work their way through and follow the heat radiating from the sheep. When they got to the sheep's.skin it would be hot and sweaty, a perfect environment for a maggot. They would then begin to eat their way into the sheep, coursing immense irritation and later death. My job was to hold the sheep while Dodd did the dirty work of cutting away all the shitty wool. Dodd was very good at showing me how to do jobs well and he always had me doing the practical side straight away. He made me do several sheep with him until I got it right.

He started by helping me to understand how to hold a sheep securely without much fuss and then how to hold the sheep and at the same time cut off the dirty wool whilst being mindful not to cut off the sheep's nipples or the tip of its private parts. Once I demonstrated to him I was capable of doing the work competently and without any assistance, he set me off doing my own thirty odd sheep under his supervision.

The first sheep in the dagging pen needed both our attention. Dodd called me over to show me what her problem was - we could see was very thin and sickly looking. Dodd told me she had been attacked by flies known as "Strike" maybe a week ago and she had gone unnoticed when we drove around checking them before. He explained she would be alive with maggots, and she was, they were all along her back and almost up to her neck. This sight made me cringe, and Mr Northern who was watching us became very angry at what the maggots had done to this poor little sheep. He told me he had a hatred for flies, a hatred I also adopted from the sight before me. Mr Northern told us to stop what we were doing for a minute whilst he came into the sheep's pen himself, something he didn't usually do any more, but the sight of this poor creature made him want to do everything he could to help her.

As he climbed over the pen he pushed me aside and took the clippers away from Dodd's hand and began clipping all the wool away from this sheep's body himself. Most of the wool just fell away because hundreds of maggots had eaten their way under the sheep's skin and killed off all the wool. As he worked with rage in his eyes many maggots fell to the ground where he would stand on them. Within no time at all, both his hands and lower arms were alive with crawling little white maggots, he tried to wipe them off with the back off clippers, most dropping away to their doom but as I watched him work I noticed a few maggots would carry on up his arms and disappeared under his shirt, he even had a few on his forehead.

There were so many maggots still on the sheep crawling everywhere very quickly, all along its back and disappearing through hundreds of tiny dark holes all over her back and upper sides. When he'd removed all the wool almost all the maggots seemed to have fallen off her or gone, he called me over and gave me a hearty demonstration on how to get the maggots back out of the sheep's body. He clasped my hand and using it as a rag rubbed it harshly on the sheep's back causing the maggots to rise up and back out of the holes. It felt like my hand was rubbing along a cheese grater as the holes had become hard and sharp. The sheep started to moan and groan at me pushing so hard on her tender and bruised flesh.

As we continued with this procedure we were both amazed to see hundreds and hundreds of the bloody things pouring out over my hand and his. Eventually he said "it's no good, she's going to die. And there is no way we can save her now, but we can kill all the f***ing maggots!"

He asked me to take the sheep away from the others and tie her against the pen while he went to his Landrover and got his gun. When he came back he had his gun in his right hand and a can of diesel fuel in his left. I stood back watching intently. I had never seen an animal shot – or anything else, for that matter. The sheep didn't look bothered that the barrel of Mr Northern gun was pointing at its head; most probably it would have been pleased, judging by the state she was in. I was feeling the tension in the air but it was not to last for long for within a few seconds....... Bang! ...... God, it was a mess. I'll spare you the details for a later story.

She went down in a tidy heap, we felt relieved for her as her plight was now over, but Mr Northern had not finished with her yet. He gave me his gun to hold while he poured diesel onto the dead sheep's back, he then knelt down onto the dirt without bothering about his tweed trousers getting blood and dirt on them and began rubbing the holes where the maggots had all disappeared.

I looked respectfully over his shoulder and watched them pouring out of all the holes, wriggling in agony as the diesel oil soaked into each and every one of them. Then, with maggots wriggling everywhere on the ground, he lit a piece of paper he had torn from a feed bag and placed it slowly onto the sheep's back. The diesel caught light and all the maggots perished. He continued until the last few came out of the holes. We then dumped the sheep into a large hessian potato sack and put her in the back of the Landrover. All in a day's work on the farm!

Every year, Mr Northern would buy a hundred or more bullocks in the autumn to fatten them up over the winter months. He would sell them sometime during late spring or maybe early summer, depending on the price at Northampton market and after they had achieved the weights he was hoping for. Mr Northern would have the bullocks distributed throughout the farm in several dilapidated barns dotted around his land. During the colder months Dodd used to load a trailer with many bags of animal feed and a large number of hay bales. He kept to a routine he followed every morning as he set off to feed the animals. When I saw Dodd loading up his trailer I would often walk across the field from our house and join up with him instead of going to school.

As a young lad of twelve I really enjoyed being with Dodd and helping in everything he did; this was man's work and I loved it all, rolling out the large and heavy round bails, then forking the straw all about the bedding area and some around the yard using just a two tongued pitch folk. I quickly began to learn about how to cope with heavy stuff and my physique quickly changed, especially in the shoulders, and my fingers started to fatten up. Moving big four legged bullocks around the yard was fun when you consider that if they had a brain inside their heads, they wouldn't run away from a skinny lad now would they! They went wherever I wanted them to go, I had full control of twenty-five one ton animals and it felt great.

I soon developed a sense of awareness when dealing with the cattle, through guidance from Dodd and the experience I had gained from working with them. Never forgetting they could be potentially dangerous if they pinned you against a wall they would kill you no doubt about it. Most often the only danger I received was when one stepped on your foot, and boy you knew it was bloody heavy then!

The first paid job Mr Northern gave me on his farm was for "corn-carting", during the summer school holidays. I had one lesson on how to drive a tractor with a two and a half ton trailer full of golden yellow corn. This was the life, driving a tractor beneath the pure blue skies on a hot summers day during August and often through into September. I couldn't drive a car or a motorbike but the power and freedom I had when driving a tractor was totally amazing for me. Tractors are serious bone shakers really, and noisy and dirty, but what else could a boy wish to drive! Most of Mr. Northern's tractors had no cabs, open tops as you might say. The couple that did have cabs didn't have a single door that could close properly anyway, so in the winter months when you were out doing field work like rolling or drilling, you were bloody freezing indeed.

Way beyond the farm and in some areas around it were many disused iron ore quarries for Corby British Steel. Several of our farm tracks ran alongside them, and one of our tracks ran past the deepest open quarry between the two main farms, which was around fifty metres in depth. One afternoon when I was using this particular track for carting straw, I saw my friend Andy walking towards me across the stubble fields, carrying on his back a bicycle. I had forgotten I had offered him a ride on the tractor one afternoon, and so there he was making his was to me. I was busy carting old rotten bales from the top farm to the bottom farm where Dodd was burning them to get rid of them.

I proudly pulled over trying to look manly to Andy. I sat looking down with my broad shoulders and my fat fingers gripping the steering wheel a little harder to make them look even fatter than they were. I asked him if he wanted to hop on the trailer and put his bike up on the bales. He jumped at the chance and off down the hill we went. He loved it, as I did in my first ride. We arrived, and Andy jumped off with his bike and stood back while I backed the trailer next to the fire and then I pulled the lever making the trailer tip the bales out. Then I drove slowly away waiting for Dodd to give me the all clear to let the trailer back down and I was free to go and collect more. My friend Andy was very impressed with me, a tractor driver!

After tipping the last load off for burning, Dodd told me to back the trailer into the barn and take off the trailer then take the tractor back to the top farm on my way home and put the keys on the hook in the tool room. I jumped into my tractor and backed it into the barn, then asked Andy to pull the "link pin" out of the trailer's drawbar when it was in the correct position so I could drive forward leaving the trailer behind. Then we went and helped Dodd burn the old bales for an hour or so.

The next three years of school was spent mainly around this environment. The quarries offered endless opportunities to explore and make discoveries, as the ground was always changing.

I am now writing my next takes from eleven years of age through to twenty one, and I'm calling it Touch-Wood

Lost and found
By
Don Howard

Copyright © 2015 Don Howard

donhowardone@gmail.com

Printed and bound in Great Britain by
Orbital Print, Sittingbourne, Kent

ORBITAL PRINT